Living Faiths

Hinduism Teacher Guide

Neera Vyas

Series Editor: Janet Dyson **Consultant:** Robert Bowie

OXFORD UNIVERSITY PRESS

Contents

Scheme of Work

This table shows links to themes in RE across the six faiths in the *Living Faiths* series, so that you can easily navigate through the series and teach by religion or by theme. The themes are organized alphabetically under the two headings, **Beliefs** and **Moral and Ethical Issues**.

	Buddhism	Christianity	Hinduism	Islam	Judaism	Sikhism
Beliefs						
Faith origins	Overview, 1.1	Overview	Overview, 2.1	Overview	Overview	Overview
Festivals / Celebrations	2.5, 2.6	3.5, 5.2	3.2, 3.3,		2.6, 3.4, 3.5, 3.7	2.6, 3.3, 3.4
Food	5.4		4.4, 4.5	3.3, 3.5	3.2	3.6, 3.7
God / Divine		1.1, 1.2, 1.3, 1.4	1.1, 1.2, 4.6	1.2	1.1, 1.3	1.1, 1.2
Key teachings	1.3, 1.4, 2.3, 2.4, 3.5	1.3, 1.6, 2.2, 4.4, 4.7	1.3, 1.4, 1.6, 3.1, 3.4, 3.5, 4.1,	1.1, 1.3, 1.5, 3.1, 3.2, 3.3, 3.4	1.2, 1.4, 1.5, 2.2, 2.5,	1.3, 1.4
Life after death	1.6, 2.6	2.5, 2.6	1.3	4.1, 4.2	4.2, 4.3	1.4
Places of worship	2.7	2.5, 3.2	2.5	2.5, 3.4	3.3	3.6, 3.8
Religious leaders	4.3, 5.5, 5.6	2.3	1.5, 2.4, 2.5, 3.1, 4.2	2.2, 2.3	1.5, 2.7	2.1, 2.2, 2.3, 2.4
Religious symbols / Dress	1.5, 3.3	3.1	2.1	3.6	3.6	3.1, 3.2
Sacred texts	2.1, 2.2,	2.1, 2.2,	2.2, 2.3	2.1, 2.4	2.1, 2.2, 2.3, 2.4	2.5
Worship	3.1, 3.2, 3.3, 3.4	1.5, 2.4, 3.2, 3.3, 3.4	3.2, 3.4, 3.6	1.3, 1.5, 3.1, 3.2, 3.3, 3.4	3.1, 3.3	3.8
Moral and Ethical Issues						
Environment / Animal rights	5.4	5.4	4.7	4.5	4.6	4.2
Evil and suffering	1.3, 1.4	4.3, 4.5	4.2, 4.3	4.3, 4.4	4.5	5.2
Fair trade	4.4	5.5	5.5			
Gender and equality / Role of women	5.2		1.5, 5.4	3.6, 5.2	5.3	5.4
Interfaith	4.3	5.6	5.6	2.2, 5.6	5.5	5.6
Medical ethics	3.6	4.2	4.2	5.4	4.1	4.4, 4.5
Relationships / Marriage / Family	5.2	5.2, 5.3	3.3, 5.3,	5.2, 5.3	5.1, 5.2	4.6
Science and religion	4.5	4.1		4.6, 5.4		4.3
Secular and atheist worldviews	4.5		1.1, 1.6	5.5	4.4, 5.5	4.3
War and peace	4.2, 5.5, 5.6	4.5, 4.6	3.1, 4.2, 5.5	4.3	5.5	5.2, 5.5
Wealth / Poverty / Charity	5.3	5.1, 5.6	3.1, 5.1,	3.2	5.4	3.5,4.1

Introduction to *Living Faiths*

How we live now

Living Faiths draws on the rich heritage of culture and diversity in twenty-first century Britain. The series focuses on case studies (shown through film and print) of young people and their families in the UK who describe how their faith affects the way they live and the moral and ethical decisions they make. The emphasis is on the personal significance of religious faith, exploring the question: What does it *mean* to be a Buddhist, Christian, Hindu, Jew, Muslim or Sikh?

This approach allows students to experience the subject fully and see its relevance to their own lives. Engagement with the case study families creates awareness of diversity, encouraging respect and enhancing social awareness. Hearing and seeing young people sharing their faith and aspects of their daily lives helps students clarify their own perspectives and reflect on their experiences, build their sense of identity and belonging, challenge prejudices and provide the knowledge and understanding to enable them to flourish in their communities.

Flexible and adaptable

Living Faiths is a series of six books, teacher guides and online resources covering Buddhism, Christianity, Hinduism, Islam, Judaism, and Sikhism. The series is designed to allow teachers the flexibility to teach by faiths or by themes, and the Scheme of Work (on page 3) provides guidance at a glance on how to teach by themes. Through structured questioning and activities, students are encouraged to make links as they learn about a range of faiths and secular world views. They are expected to identify similarities and differences within faiths, and the *Teacher Guide* further provides suggestions on how to compare and contrast between faiths. There is a strong emphasis on sources

including sacred texts, film interviews, audio and music to give students access to the lived experience of the case study families and learn what their faith means in practice.

Pedagogy

The series takes a mixed pedagogical approach inspired by the important ethnographic work that has been developed in RE in recent years. Throughout the series students are introduced to the study of faith as it is practised by believers today. The enquiry-driven focus enables them to engage with the voices and personalities of faith, getting beyond generalizations and over-simplifications, to enter into dialogue with people about their faith. Through this dialogue with living faith students will be encouraged to reflect on the experiences and beliefs of others and also on their own experiences of faith, belief and what really matters in life.

The *Living Faiths* series has been designed to engage, interest and challenge students. Each unit has an intriguing title, often a question, to capture the interest of students as soon as the lesson begins. The 'starter' activities get students thinking and discussing, drawing on their prior learning or their personal experiences as ways into the main lesson focus.

Questioning

Questioning is fundamental to good teaching and learning. Higher order questions enable students to tackle issues at a deep level and extend their thinking, develop independence in the way they learn and think and come to a fuller understanding of an idea because they have tried to explain it themselves. Bloom's Taxonomy (1956), is a useful tool for planning sequences of different types of questions of increasing difficulty to promote higher order thinking. Many of the activities are designed for pair and group discussion or for independent and small group research to promote student participation. Through the activities students will develop the ability to speculate, to raise their own questions and seek answers for themselves.

Activities

1. Do those attending the Dave memorial bhajan appear to be particularly sad or upset? Imagine you were there. Compose a social networking post describing the atmosphere.
2. 'There is no point singing to or for loved ones who have died, because they cannot hear us.' Do you agree? Prepare evidence to support your response in a class debate.
3. Hold a hot-seat event with one person taking the role of a member of the Dave family. They should respond to the statement in Activity 2.
4. What are the positive and negative aspects of spending time with your family? Work in pairs to create a pros and cons bird, with pros on one wing and cons on the other. Overall, do you value or resent spending time with your extended family?

Reflection

St Thomas Aquinas, who was a famous Roman Catholic monk and priest, said: *'Faith has to do with things that are not seen and hope with things that are not at hand.'* Do you think you can believe in things that can't be seen?

The activities are colour coded to identify three modes of thinking that are particularly valuable in the study of religion, philosophy and the broad area of social sciences.

Students are encouraged to:

- **Red: 'Think like a theologian'** these questions focus on understanding the nature of religious belief, its symbolism and spiritual significance; in the *Student Book* they are highlighted by a red question number
- **Blue: 'Think like a philosopher'** these questions focus on analysing and debating big ideas such as truth and reality; in the *Student Book* they are highlighted by a blue question number
- **Green: 'Think like a social scientist'** these questions focus on exploring and analysing why people do what they do and how belief affects action; in the *Student Book* they are highlighted by a green question number

Reflection

Reflection helps students to deepen their thinking and apply their learning about the religious beliefs and practices of others. It encourages them to explore their own beliefs in the light of what they learn, whether they are religious or not, and how they impact on personal ethics.

Thinking skills

In RE students are expected to think in increasing depth about complex issues to do with faith, beliefs, ideas and motivation. Philosophical enquiry-based approaches such as mind-mapping help students to think creatively, analytically and critically; to listen to, evaluate and respond to the views and ideas of others; to give reasons for their opinions, make connections and hypothesize; to give both sides of an argument, evaluate and draw conclusions.

Assessment

At the end of each unit there is a final assessment task which draws together students' learning.

Assessment for learning strategies are built into every unit:

- Learning objectives for each unit are written in student-friendly language and shared with students
- Students know what standards and levels they are aiming for
- Self- and peer-assessment opportunities are supported by 'I can' statements
- **AT1 Learning *about* religion** is assessed using auto-marked tests to help save you time setting questions and marking
- **AT2 Learning *from* religion** is assessed with step-by-step tasks and support materials. These use effective assessment for learning strategies to help students recognize next steps and improve performance.

We hope that you will enjoy using this series to bring real families of faith into the classroom, and to introduce students to the liveliness and relevance of religious education.

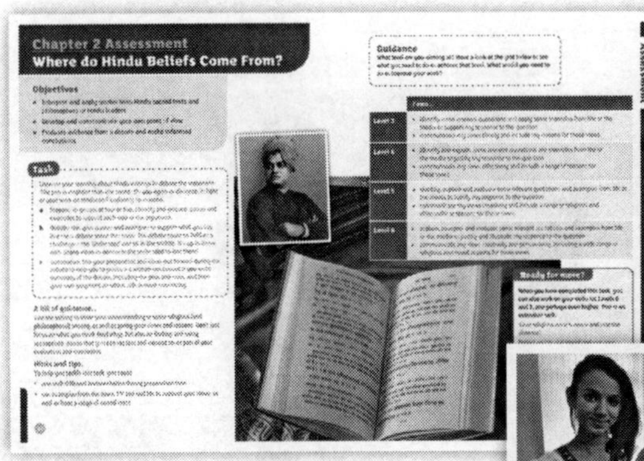

Janet Dyson
(Series Editor)

Robert Bowie
(Series Consultant)

About this Series

Living Faiths Hinduism is one of six Religious Education Student Books covering the following major faiths: Buddhism, Christianity, Hinduism, Islam, Judaism, and Sikhism. This series fully integrates real-life film clips and other exciting multimedia resources on the *Oxbox Online* with the *Student Books* and *Teacher Guides*, so your lessons can be delivered easily and seamlessly.

The series components

The series consist of:

For students

- Six *Student Books* (and/or six *Online Student Books*)
- Six *OxBox Online* Lessons, Resources and Assessments.

For teachers

- Six *Teacher Guides*
- Six *OxBox Online* Lessons, Resources and Assessments (includes teacher access to the accompanying *Online Student Book*).

Student Book

The ***Living Faiths Hinduism Student Book*** uses **real-life case studies** to encourage students to ask questions, actively engage with **moral** and **ethical** issues, and reflect on the relevance of RE.

Starter activities spark your students' interest in new topics

The 'Reflection' feature helps your students to consider beliefs and practices of others, and how they link to their own lives and beliefs

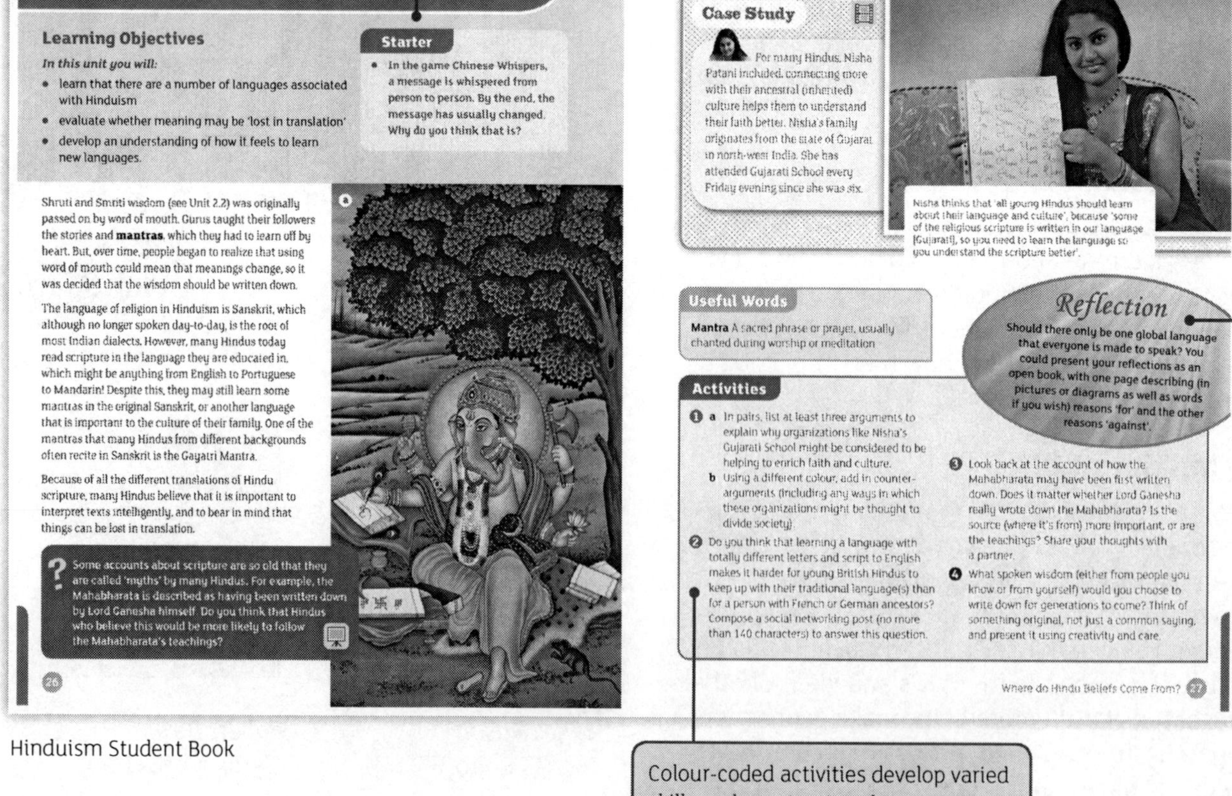

2.3 What does it Mean? Intelligent Interpretation

Learning Objectives

In this unit you will:

- learn that there are a number of languages associated with Hinduism
- evaluate whether meaning may be 'lost in translation'
- develop an understanding of how it feels to learn new languages.

Starter

- In the game Chinese Whispers, a message is whispered from person to person. By the end, the message has usually changed. Why do you think that is?

Shruti and Smriti wisdom (see Unit 2.2) was originally passed on by word of mouth. Gurus taught their followers the stories and **mantras**, which they had to learn off by heart. But, over time, people began to realize that using word of mouth could mean that meanings change, so it was decided that the wisdom should be written down.

The language of religion in Hinduism is Sanskrit, which although no longer spoken day-to-day, is the root of most Indian dialects. However, many Hindus today read scripture in the language they are educated in, which might be anything from English to Portuguese to Mandarin! Despite this, they may still learn some mantras in the original Sanskrit, or another language that is important to the culture of their family. One of the mantras that many Hindus from different backgrounds often recite in Sanskrit is the Gayatri Mantra.

Because of all the different translations of Hindu scripture, many Hindus believe that it is important to interpret texts intelligently, and to bear in mind that things can be lost in translation.

? Some accounts about scripture are so old that they are called 'myths' by many Hindus. For example, the Mahabharata is described as having been written down by Lord Ganesha himself. Do you think that Hindus who believe this would be more likely to follow the Mahabharata's teachings?

26

Case Study

For many Hindus, Nisha Patani included, connecting more with their ancestral (inherited) culture helps them to understand their faith better. Nisha's family originates from the state of Gujarat in north-west India. She has attended Gujarati School every Friday evening since she was six.

Nisha thinks that 'all young Hindus should learn about their language and culture', because 'some of the religious scripture is written in our language [Gujarati], so you need to learn the language so you understand the scripture better'.

Useful Words

Mantra A sacred phrase or prayer, usually chanted during worship or meditation

Reflection

Should there only be one global language that everyone is made to speak? You could present your reflections as an open book, with one page describing (in pictures or diagrams as well as words if you wish) reasons 'for' and the other reasons 'against'.

Activities

1. **a** In pairs, list at least three arguments to explain why organizations like Nisha's Gujarati School might be considered to be helping to enrich faith and culture.
   b Using a different colour, add in counter-arguments (including any ways in which these organizations might be thought to divide society).
2. Do you think that learning a language with totally different letters and script to English makes it harder for young British Hindus to keep up with their traditional language(s) than for a person with French or German ancestors? Compose a social networking post (no more than 140 characters) to answer this question.
3. Look back at the account of how the Mahabharata may have been first written down. Does it matter whether Lord Ganesha really wrote down the Mahabharata? Is the source (where it's from) more important, or are the teachings? Share your thoughts with a partner.
4. What spoken wisdom (either from people you know or from yourself) would you choose to write down for generations to come? Think of something original, not just a common saying, and present it using creativity and care.

Where do Hindu Beliefs Come From? 27

Hinduism Student Book

Colour-coded activities develop varied skills and are structured to encourage progression and allow differentiation

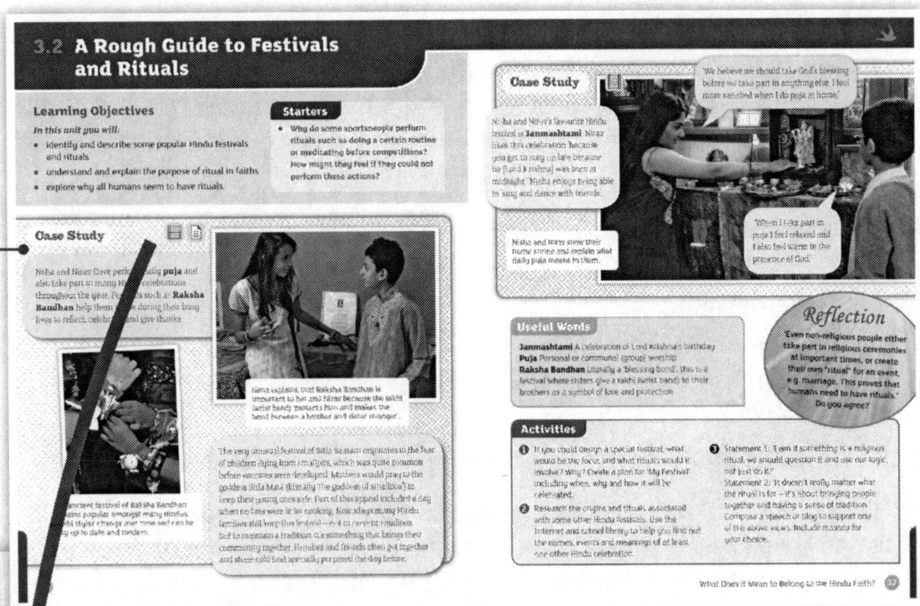

Case studies provide first-hand experience of real Hindu families talking about their faith

Hinduism Student Book

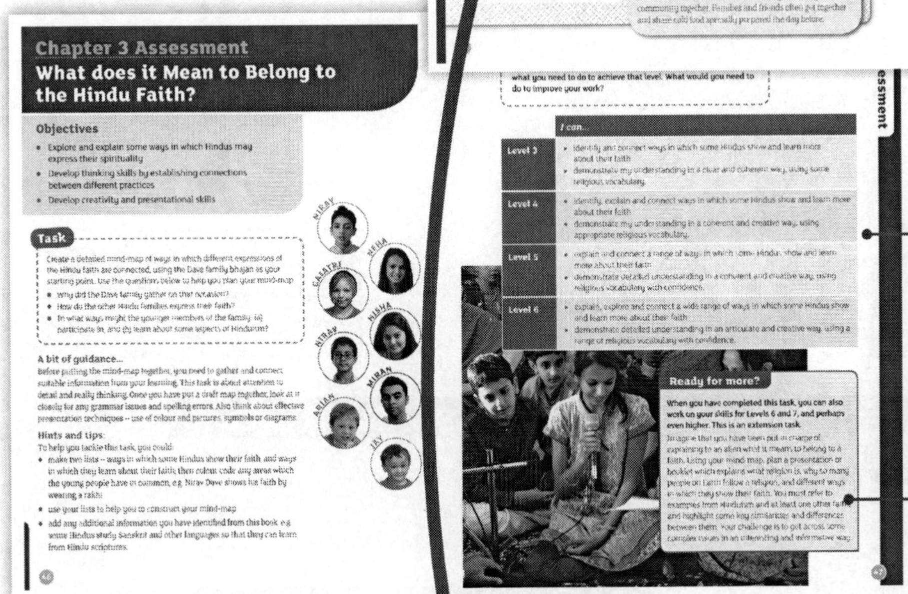

There is an assessment spread for every chapter in the *Student Book* to help students determine what level they are aiming for and make progress

Extensions tasks within assessments challenge more able students

Case studies are linked directly to films on the *OxBox Online* and are marked with film icons on each page

Hinduism OxBox Online

Authors

Experienced RE Consultant **Janet Dyson** and well-known author and PGCE tutor **Robert Bowie** lead the author **Neera Vyas**, who is an experienced RE teacher.

Using this Book

Teacher Guide

The ***Living Faiths Hinduism Teacher Guide*** aims to save you time and effort. It provides **full support** and guidance for the *Hinduism Student Book*, including **practical tasks** and **creative suggestions** for incorporating differentiation into your teaching.

What it provides

For each chapter of the student book, this book provides:

- a chapter overview
- help at a glance for each unit
- further suggestions for class and homework
- an assessment overview.

It also has a **Glossary** at the back, covering the RE terms students will meet.

Please turn to the **Contents List** on page 2 to see how this book is structured. While the Living Faiths series is organized by religion, a **Scheme of Work** on page 3 is also provided to help you teach RE **by themes**.

Find out more about the four main components below.

The chapter overview

This is your introduction to the corresponding *Student Book* chapter.

Shows how the *Student Book* chapter relates to the KS3 RE Programme of Study (non-statutory)

Reminds you that some lessons, including starters and plenaries, will need resources prepared in advance

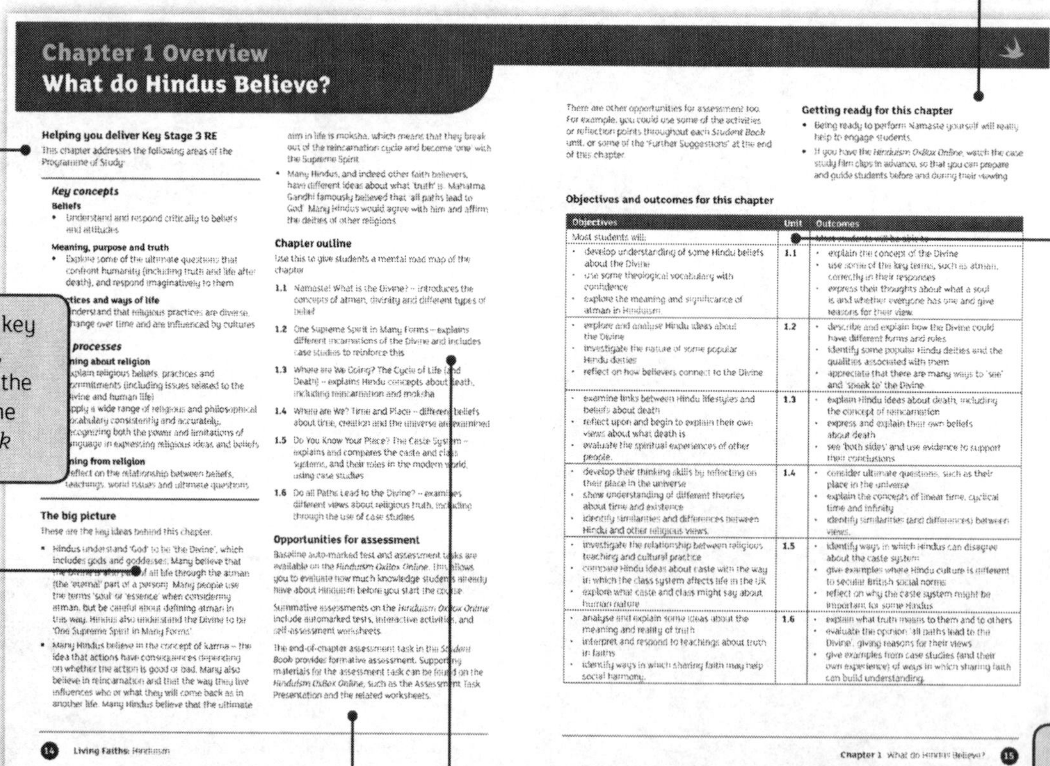

Sets out the key ideas within, and behind, the chapter in the *Student Book*

Points you to the assessment material for the chapter (summative and formal assessments, and related resources)

Gives a brief summary of what's covered in the *Student Book* chapter. It will help you give students a road map for the chapter

Sets out the objectives and outcomes for the chapter, and the corresponding unit numbers

Help at a glance for each unit

These pages give comprehensive help for each unit of the *Student Book*.

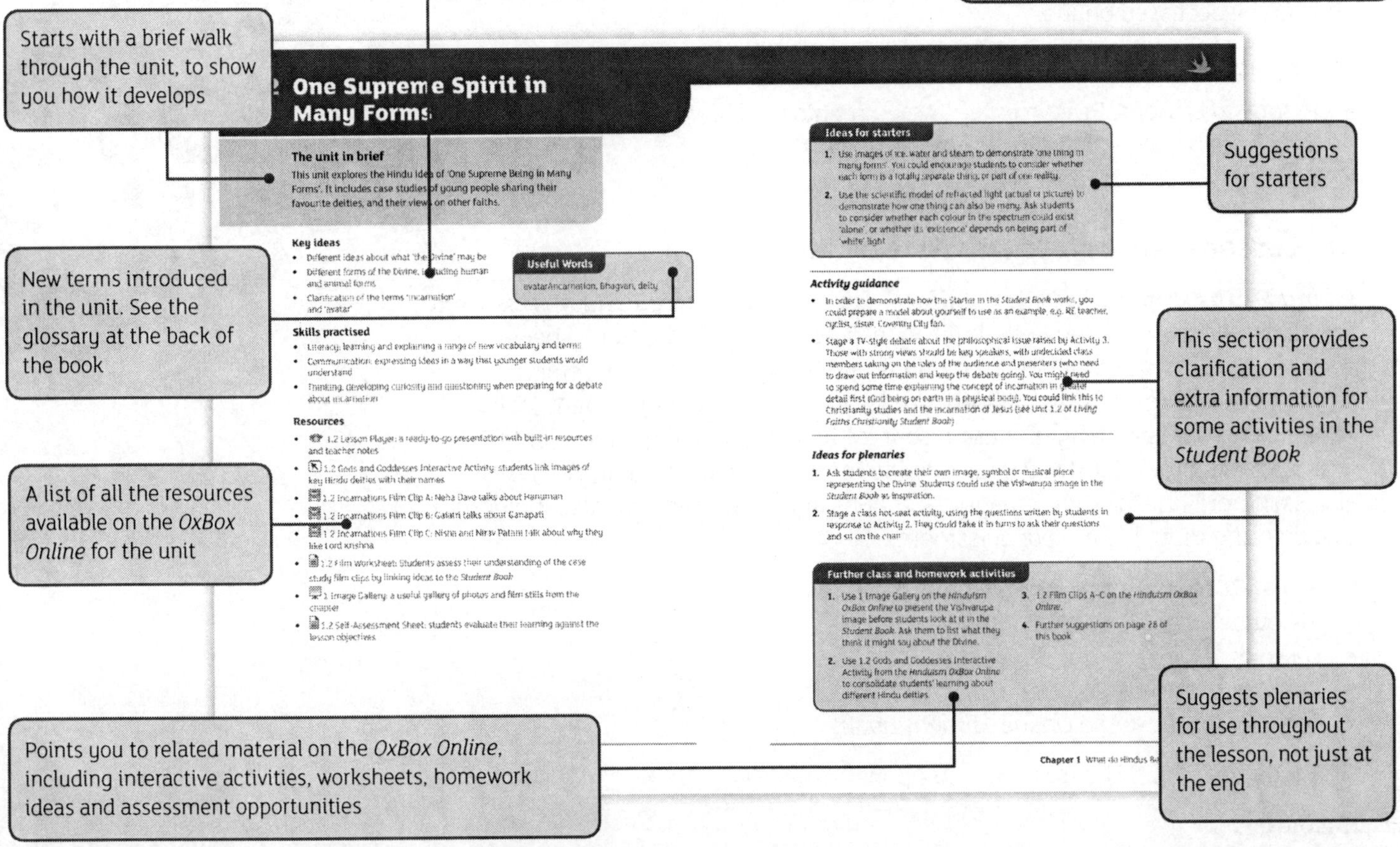

Further suggestions for class and homework

These pages give a bank of further suggestions for class and homework.

They have been graded *, ** or *** according to level of difficulty.

These suggestions are addressed directly to students.

1.1 Namaste! What is the Divine?

1 What do we really mean by 'respect'? Share your reflections as a blog, poem, or piece of art. ***

2 Investigate other forms of greetings from a range of faiths and cultures. */**/***

1.4 Where are We? Time and Place

1 Find three different creation stories or theories from different belief systems (including one non-religious). Identify what they have in common, and what they differ on. Which is the most convincing and why? ***

2 Consider the concept from *The Hitch Hiker's*

Suggestions are graded, but some are suitable for all levels, and differentiated by outcome

The assessment overview

This section introduces you to the end-of-chapter assessment task from the *Student Book*, and describes the support materials available for the chapter.

Assessment in the *Student Book*

You will find an assessment task at the end of every chapter which focuses on AT2. In this chapter, the task asks students to explore, evaluate and reflect on the purpose of life, both from a Hindu perspective and their own point of view.

In the *Student Book* (and on the supporting worksheets), you'll find guidance about levels of assessment that you can use to help your students understand what their work should include. You could ask them to use these criteria for self- or peer-assessment once they've completed the task.

Living Faiths Assessment

Student Book

- Assessment Task
- Levels Guidance

OxBox Online

- Auto-Marked Test
- Assessment Task Presentation
- Assessment Worksheets

The purpose of the end-of-chapter assessment task from the *Student Book* is summarized

You can see all the assessment materials available for the chapter at a glance

OxBox Online

Living Faiths Hinduism OxBox Online is packed full of guided support and ideas for running and creating effective lessons on Hinduism. It's intuitive to use, customizable, and can be accessed online.

It consists of:

- Hinduism Lessons, Resources and Assessments (includes teacher access to the accompanying *Online Student Book*)
- *Hinduism Online Student Book*.

Lessons, Resources and Assessment

Living Faiths Hinduism OxBox Online – Lessons, Resources and Assessment provides over one hundred lively built-in resources, including unique specially commissioned films of real Hindu families practising their faiths, interactive activities, ready-to-go lesson presentations, and supported assessment tasks. You can even **adapt** many of these resources to suit you and your students' individual needs, and **upload** your existing resources so everything can be accessed from one location. Image collections and audio clips are also included to help bring RE to life in your classroom.

Lessons, Resources and Assessment provides:

- Resources
- Lessons
- Assessment and Markbook
- Teacher access to the *Online Student Book*.

Find out more about the four main components below.

Resources

Click on the **Resources tab** at the top of the screen to access the full list of *Living Faiths Hinduism* resources.

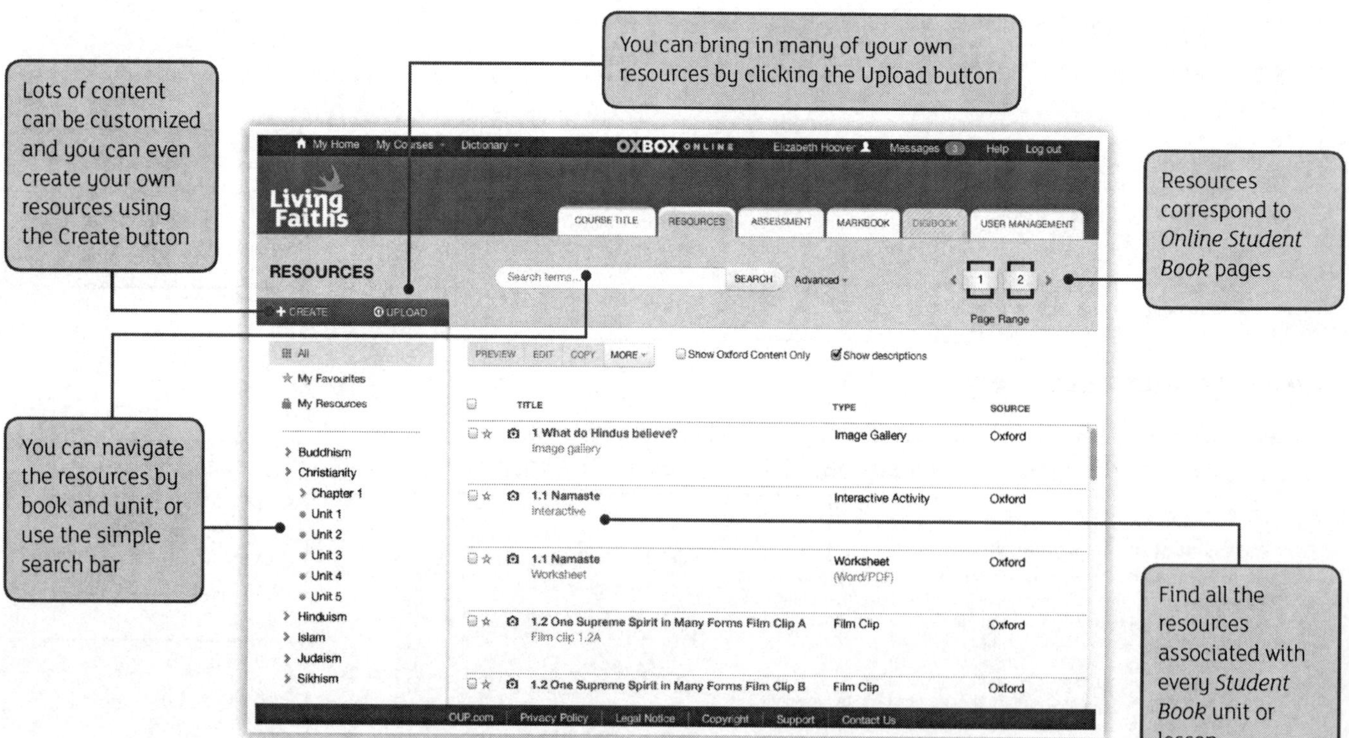

Hinduism OxBox Online

The Resources section has more than:

20 Film clips: Specially commissioned films help your students to actively engage with RE through watching real Hindu families practise their faith and to explore the diversity within Hinduism.

10 Audio clips: Specially commissioned music and narrated sources help bring RE alive in your classroom.

70 Worksheets: Creative worksheets that help provide differentiation/extension material for each unit, and film worksheets to help students assess their own learning of the case study film clips and link ideas back to the *Student Book* unit. They are provided as PDFs, which you can print off and photocopy, and as Word files, which you can amend to suit your students' needs.

30 Interactive activities: Various types of activities are available for each unit as short main activities, plenaries or summative assessments. They can also be used for independent study. Most of these activities are auto-marked to help you save time marking.

80 Images: An image gallery with captions is provided for each chapter so you can easily enlarge any photo or artwork from the *Student Book* on screen and use it as a discussion starter, use them in your own worksheets, or give them to students to use in class or homework activities.

OxBox Online Resources are fully integrated with the *Student Book*:

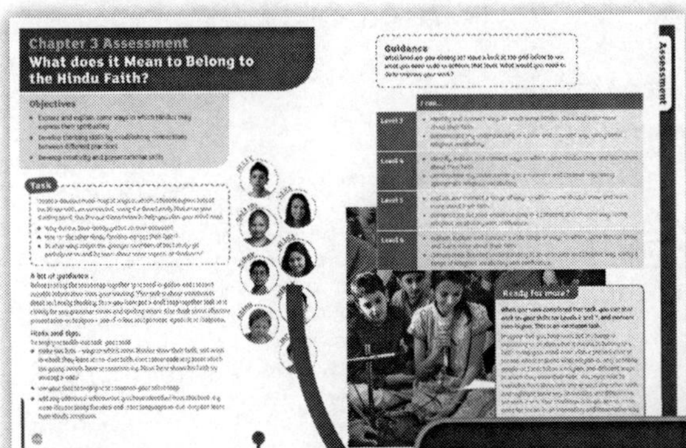

Hinduism Student Book

Real Hindu families are featured in the *Student Book* and you can find the specially commissioned films related to *Student Book* units on *OxBox Online*

Use the accompanying film worksheets to help your students consolidate what they have learnt

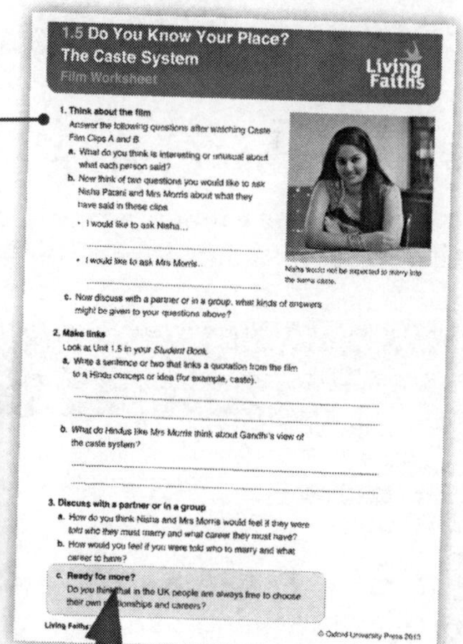

All the resources and assessments are **fully integrated** with the *Hinduism Student Book*

OxBox Online

Lesson presentations

Click on the **Lessons tab** to access the full list of *Living Faiths Hinduism* lessons and notes.

Ready-to-play lesson presentations complement every unit in the book. Each lesson presentation is easy to launch, and features unit objectives, the related starters, worksheets, film and interactive resources, and closes with a plenary activity or reflection. You can further **personalize** the lessons by adding in your own resources and notes. Your lessons and notes can be accessed by your whole department, and they are a great time-saver and **ideal for non-specialist** teachers and cover lessons.

Resources are built into each lesson presentation so all the relevant activities, film clips and worksheets are ready to launch

The resources you want to use can also be rearranged and launched in sequence to suit your classroom needs

Every lesson is accompanied by teacher notes to fully support your lesson delivery

Slide 2

Activity Guidance: Read through Unit 1.2 in the *Student Book*. Students can use the example spider diagram (on Slide 2) of the 'roles' the author of *Living Faiths: Hinduism* assigns herself to inform their own diagram, or you could create your own example, if you prefer.

Note: This starter is taken from the *Student Book*.

Slide 3

Interactive Activity: The students can use the images in the *Student Book* to help inform them which deity is which. Some of the information in the film clips may also help them with this activity.

Slide 4

Film Clips: Ask students to note key features of the deities chosen as 'favourites' in the case study films. Any notes they make will help them complete the Interactive Activity for this unit. For 1.2 Incarnations Film Clip C, you could ask students to discuss whether they are surprised by the views expressed or whether they expected them. Do they agree or disagree, and why?

Worksheet: Students can work through both individually and in groups to answer the questions on the worksheet.

Assessment and Markbook

Click on the **Assessment tab** to find a wide range of assessment materials to help you deliver a varied, motivating, and effective assessment programme.

A markbook and reporting function help keep everything you need in one place

Learning about religion (AT1) is assessed using auto-marked tests to help save you time

Learning from religion (AT2) is assessed with step-by-step tasks and support materials

The Assessment section provides:

- **2 baseline tests:** These tests cover both **Attainment Target 1** (learning *about* religion) and **Attainment Target 2** (learning *from* religion), and they can help you to quickly assess the prior RE knowledge that your new KS3 students may have.
- **5 auto-marked tests**: Each end-of-chapter auto-marked test assesses **AT1**. The marks are automatically reported in the **Markbook tab**.
- **30 self-assessment worksheets**: Self-assessment worksheets help students to self- or peer-evaluate the skills they have learnt from each unit.
- **5 assessment task presentations**: Each end-of-chapter assessment task in the *Student Book*, which assesses **AT2**, has a front-of-class presentation for you to use to help guide students towards understanding and analysing what the question/task is asking of them. You can lead students through this step-by-step presentation and help them decide how to prepare to answer the question.
- **15 assessment worksheets**: These worksheets complement the assessment tasks in the *Student Book* and the assessment task presentations. They recap the task, provide a self-evaluation chart, and space for students to prepare their work.

A **Markbook** with reporting function completes the *OxBox Online* assessment package, so you can keep track of all your students' test results and assessment scores. This includes both the automarked tests and work that need to be marked by you. It is also easy to import class registers and create user accounts for all your students.

Online Student Book

The ***Hinduism Online Student Book*** provides you with an on-screen version of the *Student Book* for you to use on your whiteboard with the whole class.

Teacher access to the *Online Student Book* is **automatically available** as part of the Lessons, Resources and Assessment package. You can also choose to buy access for your students.

Both teacher and student access include a simple bank of tools so you can personalize the book and take notes.

It can be accessed on other devices, such as tablets.

Zoom in and spotlight any part of the text

Use different tools such as Sticky Notes, Bookmarks and Pencil features to personalize each page

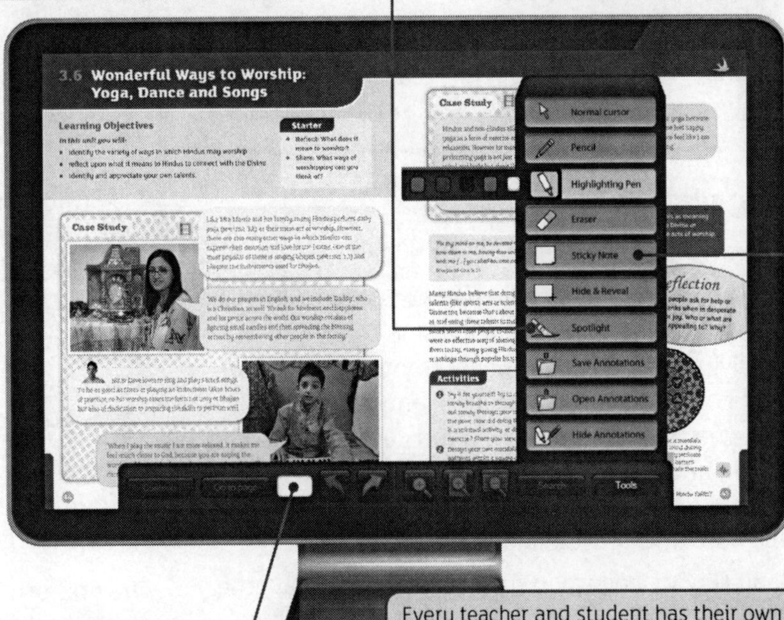

Navigate around the book quickly with the contents menu, keyword search or page number search

Every teacher and student has their own digital notebook for use within their *Online Student Book*. You can even choose to share some of your notes with your students, or hide them from view – all student notes are accessible to themselves only

Chapter 1 Overview
What do Hindus Believe?

Helping you deliver Key Stage 3 RE

This chapter addresses the following areas of the Programme of Study:

Key concepts

Beliefs

- Understand and respond critically to beliefs and attitudes

Meaning, purpose and truth

- Explore some of the ultimate questions that confront humanity (including truth and life after death), and respond imaginatively to them

Practices and ways of life

- Understand that religious practices are diverse, change over time and are influenced by cultures

Key processes

Learning about religion

- Explain religious beliefs, practices and commitments (including issues related to the Divine and human life)
- Apply a wide range of religious and philosophical vocabulary consistently and accurately, recognizing both the power and limitations of language in expressing religious ideas and beliefs

Learning from religion

- Reflect on the relationship between beliefs, teachings, world issues and ultimate questions

The big picture

These are the key ideas behind this chapter:

- Hindus understand 'God' to be 'the Divine', which includes gods and goddesses. Many believe that the Divine is also part of all life through the atman (the 'eternal' part of a person). Many people use the terms 'soul' or 'essence' when considering atman, but be careful about defining atman in this way. Hindus also understand the Divine to be 'One Supreme Spirit in Many Forms'.
- Many Hindus believe in the concept of karma – the idea that actions have consequences depending on whether the action is good or bad. Many also believe in reincarnation and that the way they live influences who or what they will come back as in another life. Many Hindus believe that the ultimate aim in life is moksha, which means that they break out of the reincarnation cycle and become 'one' with the Supreme Spirit.
- Many Hindus, and indeed other faith believers, have different ideas about what 'truth' is. Mahatma Gandhi famously believed that 'all paths lead to God'. Many Hindus would agree with him and affirm the deities of other religions.

Chapter outline

Use this to give students a mental road map of the chapter:

1.1 Namaste! What is the Divine? – introduces the concepts of atman, divinity and different types of belief

1.2 One Supreme Spirit in Many Forms – explains different incarnations of the Divine and includes case studies to reinforce this

1.3 Where are We Going? The Cycle of Life (and Death) – explains Hindu concepts about death, including reincarnation and moksha

1.4 Where are We? Time and Place – different beliefs about time, creation and the universe are examined

1.5 Do You Know Your Place? The Caste System – explains and compares the caste and class systems, and their roles in the modern world, using case studies

1.6 Do all Paths Lead to the Divine? – examines different views about religious truth, including through the use of case studies

Opportunities for assessment

Baseline auto-marked test and assessment tasks are available on the *Hinduism OxBox Online*. This allows you to evaluate how much knowledge students already have about Hinduism before you start the course.

Summative assessments on the *Hinduism OxBox Online* include automarked tests, interactive activities, and self-assessment worksheets.

The end-of-chapter assessment task in the *Student Book* provides formative assessment. Supporting materials for the assessment task can be found on the *Hinduism OxBox Online*, such as the Assessment Task Presentation and the related worksheets.

There are other opportunities for assessment too. For example, you could use some of the activities or reflection points throughout each *Student Book* unit, or some of the 'Further Suggestions' at the end of this chapter.

Getting ready for this chapter

- Being ready to perform Namaste yourself will really help to engage students.
- If you have the *Hinduism OxBox Online*, watch the case study film clips in advance, so that you can prepare and guide students before and during their viewing.

Objectives and outcomes for this chapter

Objectives	Unit	Outcomes
Most students will:		Most students will be able to:
• develop understanding of some Hindu beliefs about the Divine • use some theological vocabulary with confidence • explore the meaning and significance of atman in Hinduism.	**1.1**	• explain the concept of the Divine • use some of the key terms, such as atman, correctly in their responses • express their thoughts about what a soul is and whether everyone has one and give reasons for their view.
• explore and analyse Hindu ideas about the Divine • investigate the nature of some popular Hindu deities • reflect on how believers connect to the Divine.	**1.2**	• describe and explain how the Divine could have different forms and roles • identify some popular Hindu deities and the qualities associated with them • appreciate that there are many ways to 'see' and 'speak to' the Divine.
• examine links between Hindu lifestyles and beliefs about death • reflect upon and begin to explain their own views about what death is • evaluate the spiritual experiences of other people.	**1.3**	• explain Hindu ideas about death, including the concept of reincarnation • express and explain their own beliefs about death • see 'both sides' and use evidence to support their conclusions.
• develop their thinking skills by reflecting on their place in the universe • show understanding of different theories about time and existence • identify similarities and differences between Hindu and other religious views.	**1.4**	• consider ultimate questions, such as their place in the universe • explain the concepts of linear time, cyclical time and infinity • identify similarities (and differences) between views.
• investigate the relationship between religious teaching and cultural practice • compare Hindu ideas about caste with the way in which the class system affects life in the UK • explore what caste and class might say about human nature.	**1.5**	• identify ways in which Hindus can disagree about the caste system • give examples where Hindu culture is different to secular British social norms • reflect on why the caste system might be important for some Hindus.
• analyse and explain some ideas about the meaning and reality of truth • interpret and respond to teachings about truth in faiths • identify ways in which sharing faith may help social harmony.	**1.6**	• explain what truth means to them and to others • evaluate the opinion 'all paths lead to the Divine', giving reasons for their views • give examples from case studies (and their own experience) of ways in which sharing faith can build understanding.

1.1 Namaste! What is the Divine?

The unit in brief

This unit begins with the greeting 'Namaste', which is used as a hook to explain Hindu beliefs about atman and the Divine. Key terms about belief are explained in detail as a basis for future learning.

Key ideas

- The concept of atman
- Different belief systems and ideas about what the Divine is
- Ways in which humans/living things and the Divine may be connected

Useful Words

atheism, atman, the Divine, monotheism, pantheism, pluralism, polytheism, soul

Skills practised

- Literacy: learning key words and rewording quotes from sacred texts
- Thinking: creating a mind-map of some Hindu beliefs about the Divine
- Research: preparing arguments for a debate

Resources

- 1.1 Quotations Worksheet: students analyse scriptural quotations about atman and the Divine
- 1.1 Lesson Player: a ready-to-go presentation with built-in resources and teacher notes
- 1.1 Divine Beliefs Interactive Activity: students drag key words to their definitions
- 1 Image Gallery: a useful gallery of photos and film stills from the chapter
- 1.1 Self-Assessment Sheet: students evaluate their learning against the lesson objectives

Ideas for starters

1. Use the Starter from the *Student Book*.

a) Ask students, in pairs or groups, to demonstrate their responses to the first starter question: 'How do you normally greet people?'. They could act out their greetings to one another.

b) With less confident groups, you could start by sharing how you personally greet people and explain why. With more confident groups, you could share how you personally greet people afterwards, with an explanation.

c) Then ask each group to choose three greetings and ask the second starter question: 'Why do you use those ways?' Feed back as a class.

2. You could use images or clips of people greeting each other in different ways as a follow on from, or instead of, sharing your own ways of greeting.

Activity guidance

Students are asked in the *Student Book* to reword quotations from Hindu scripture into student speak. You could ask them to do this task in small groups. Once they have completed the task, feed back and compare the similarities and differences between the groups. Discuss possible reasons for them. Alternatively, students could use 1.1 Quotations Worksheet to complete this activity.

Ideas for plenaries

1. Use the Reflection from the *Student Book*. You could ask students to share and compare their thoughts in twos or threes.
2. Search online for the video clip of Pastor Eddie D. Smith talking about 'The Meaning of Namaste'. The Pastor says that the world would be a better and safer place if everyone showed the love and respect of Namaste when they greet each other. Show students the video and ask them whether or not they agree.
3. Ask students to perform and explain Namaste to each other in pairs.
4. Ask students to think of other words that contain 'mono', 'poly' and 'pan' to reinforce their understanding of these key terms.
5. Ask students to share and explain their responses to the mind-map activity. This is a useful opportunity for peer assessment.

Further class and homework activities

1. Students should learn the Useful Words and definitions explored in this *Student Book* unit for a quick quiz next lesson.
2. Before asking students to attempt 1.1 Divine Beliefs Interactive Activity, you could show them pictures of a monorail, polygon and panoramic view.
3. 1.1 Divine Beliefs Interactive Activity on the *Hinduism OxBox Online*.
4. 1.1 Quotations Worksheet on the *Hinduism OxBox Online*.
5. Further suggestions on page 28 of this book.

1.2 One Supreme Spirit in Many Forms

The unit in brief

This unit explores the Hindu idea of 'One Supreme Being in Many Forms'. It includes case studies of young people sharing their favourite deities, and their views on other faiths.

Key ideas

- Different ideas about what 'the Divine' may be
- Different forms of the Divine, including human and animal forms
- Clarification of the terms 'incarnation' and 'avatar'

Useful Words

avatar/incarnation, Bhagvan, deity

Skills practised

- Literacy: learning and explaining a range of new vocabulary and terms
- Communication: expressing ideas in a way that younger students would understand
- Thinking: developing curiosity and questioning when preparing for a debate about incarnation

Resources

- 1.2 Lesson Player: a ready-to-go presentation with built-in resources and teacher notes
- 1.2 Gods and Goddesses Interactive Activity: students link images of key Hindu deities with their names
- 1.2 Incarnations Film Clip A: Neha Dave talks about Hanuman
- 1.2 Incarnations Film Clip B: Gaiatri talks about Ganapati
- 1.2 Incarnations Film Clip C: Nisha and Nirav Patani talk about why they like Lord Krishna
- 1.2 Film Worksheet: Students assess their understanding of the case study film clips by linking ideas to the *Student Book*
- 1 Image Gallery: a useful gallery of photos and film stills from the chapter
- 1.2 Self-Assessment Sheet: students evaluate their learning against the lesson objectives

Ideas for starters

1. Use images of ice, water and steam to demonstrate 'one thing in many forms'. You could encourage students to consider whether each form is a totally separate thing, or part of one reality.
2. Use the scientific model of refracted light (actual or picture) to demonstrate how one thing can also be many. Ask students to consider whether each colour in the spectrum could exist 'alone', or whether its 'existence' depends on being part of 'white' light.

Activity guidance

- In order to demonstrate how the Starter in the *Student Book* works, you could prepare a model about yourself to use as an example, e.g. RE teacher, cyclist, sister, Coventry City fan.
- Stage a TV-style debate about the philosophical issue raised by Activity 3. Those with strong views should be key speakers, with undecided class members taking on the roles of the audience and presenters (who need to draw out information and keep the debate going). You might need to spend some time explaining the concept of incarnation in greater detail first (God being on earth in a physical body). You could link this to Christianity studies and the incarnation of Jesus (see Unit 1.2 of *Living Faiths Christianity Student Book*).

Ideas for plenaries

1. Ask students to create their own image, symbol or musical piece representing the Divine. Students could use the Vishvarupa image in the *Student Book* as inspiration.
2. Stage a class hot-seat activity, using the questions written by students in response to Activity 2. They could take it in turns to ask their questions and sit on the chair.

Further class and homework activities

1. Use 1 Image Gallery on the *Hinduism OxBox Online* to present the Vishvarupa image before students look at it in the *Student Book*. Ask them to list what they think it might say about the Divine.
2. Use 1.2 Gods and Goddesses Interactive Activity from the *Hinduism OxBox Online* to consolidate students' learning about different Hindu deities.
3. 1.2 Film Clips A–C on the *Hinduism OxBox Online*.
4. Further suggestions on page 28 of this book.

1.3 Where are We Going? The Cycle of Life (and Death)

The unit in brief

This unit investigates beliefs about life after death. The Hindu concept of reincarnation is explained and evaluated. Students are also asked to consider their own beliefs about death.

Key ideas

- What death means
- The possibility of an afterlife
- Reincarnation and what many Hindus believe about life after death

Useful Words

afterlife, moksha, narg, reincarnation, swarg

Skills practised

- Thinking: questioning and evaluating spiritual experiences
- Reflecting: considering what factors might influence our own views on death
- Communicating: working in pairs or groups to compare ideas

Resources

- 1.3 Poem Audio Clip: a reading of the poem "Do not stand at my grave and weep"
- 1.3 Reincarnation Worksheet: students assess real-life accounts of reincarnation
- 1.3 Lesson Player: a ready-to-go presentation with built-in resources and teacher notes
- 1.3 Afterlife Interactive Activity A: students fill the gaps in a paragraph summarising the unit
- 1.3 Afterlife Interactive Activity B: students assess arguments for and against life after death
- 1 Image Gallery: a useful gallery of photos and film stills from the chapter
- 1.3 Self-Assessment Sheet: students evaluate their learning against the lesson objectives

Ideas for starters

1. Use the Starter from the *Student Book*. An alternative poem/ narrative or range of narratives to illustrate views about death could be used.
2. Research famous epitaphs and discuss with students what they say about death.
3. Use sections (read aloud or film clips) from *Harry Potter*, featuring the 'spirit' of his parents and/or the ghosts. Ask students to discuss their understanding of 'spirit' and of 'ghosts' as a lead-in to the key question: 'What is death?'.
4. Read aloud a section from the book *Mort* by Terry Pratchett, where Death explains that what happens when people die is whatever they expect or believe will happen. Students discuss their response and share their own beliefs about death.

Activity guidance

This unit refers to other beliefs about death and the afterlife. To compare with other faiths, see Chapter 2 in the *Christianity Student Book* or Unit 1.6 in the *Buddhism Student Book*.

Ideas for plenaries

1. Use the Reflection from the *Student Book*.
2. Ask students to design a survey to find out what death means to other people. They should come up with their own questions but, as a general guide, they could include the options of: Nothing, Heaven, Heaven or Hell, Reincarnation, Other (describe), Not Sure.
   - **a)** Students could either survey class members, or ask others as homework.
   - **b)** They could also use numeracy skills to create bar graphs of their results.
   - **c)** A useful starter for the next lesson would be to analyse the bar graphs and survey results.
3. As a follow-up or alternative to 1.3 Reincarnation Worksheet, ask students to choose a real-life account of a near-death experience, or someone who claims to know they have been reincarnated. You might want to find these accounts online in advance and ask students to choose one.
   - **a)** Ask them to go through the account noting evidence and examples for and against the issue of life after death or reincarnation.
   - **b)** Ask: 'What is convincing about the account? What is unconvincing? What factors might have influenced this person? What might a Hindu say is happening here?'
   - **c)** Ask students, in groups, to use their notes and reflections to prepare a news report of their own – either presented 'live' to the class, or recorded as an audio or filmed report. You could suggest that students use the skill sets within each group wisely to decide who prepares scripts, who speaks, who acts as an expert or witness and so on.
4. Search online for the clip on the BBC website entitled 'Reincarnation: you only live twice?' Use this to consolidate students' understanding of reincarnation. Ask the following questions: 'What do Hindus believe will happen to them if they lead a good or bad life? How does this impact on their day-to-day lives?' For more able students, you could ask them to make comparisons with the other religions you are studying.

Further class and homework activities

1. Students should learn the Useful Words and definitions explored in this *Student Book* unit for a quick quiz next lesson.
2. Play students 1.3 Poem Audio Clip while they read the poem in the book. You may wish to play the clip first, before asking them to look at the words more closely in the book.
3. 1.3 Afterlife Interactive Activities A and B on the *Hinduism OxBox Online*.
4. 1.3 Reincarnation Worksheet on the *Hinduism OxBox Online*.
5. Further suggestions on page 28 of this book.

1.4 Where are We? Time and Place

The unit in brief

This unit explores some Hindu beliefs about existence and time, including how the universe came to be and the place of humans within it.

Key ideas

- What various religious traditions believe about the importance of human beings in relation to the universe
- Whether time is linear or cyclical
- Hindu beliefs and theories about creation

Useful Words

cyclical time, eternal, infinite, linear time,

Skills practised

- Thinking: comparing and evaluating different beliefs and theories
- Enquiry: exploring what is meant by time and creation
- Communication: expressing own views and those of others when creating a dramatic recital of Hindu scripture
- Numeracy: understanding the vastness of space compared to objects on Earth
- Reflecting: considering our place in the universe

Resources

- 1.4 Starter Film Clip A: a film of a sandy beach to accompany the Starter activity
- 1.4 Starter Film Clip B: a film of a crowded sports stadium to accompany the Starter activity
- 1.4 Upanishads Audio Clip: a reading from the Maitri Upanishad about creation and universes
- 1.4 Creation Worksheet: students storyboard their own creation story
- 1.4 Audio Handout: contains the passage from the Maitri Upanishad about creation and universes
- 1.4 Lesson Player: a ready-to-go presentation with built-in resources and teacher notes
- 1.4 Cyclical or Linear Interactive Activity: students attribute ideas about time to Hinduism or Christianity
- 1 Image Gallery: a useful gallery of photos and film stills from the chapter
- 1.4 Self-Assessment Sheet: students evaluate their learning against the lesson objectives

Ideas for starters

1. Highlight numeracy aspects by providing a visual ratio example, e.g. 'How many tennis balls would it take to fill this room? The world? Our universe?'
2. Present the infinity symbol(∞) on a whiteboard or paper. Ask students to discuss what it represents and how it might connect to Hinduism.

Activity guidance

- Once students have completed Activity **1** in the *Student Book*, you could ask the small groups to perform their dramatic recitals to the rest of the class. A spokesperson could summarize their group's discussions afterwards.
- Once students have written their own versions of a creation story (Activity **3** or 1.3 Creation Worksheet), you could ask for volunteers to share them with the rest of the class. Class members could ask questions and discuss the ideas that are suggested.
- You could compare and contrast the Hindu concept of time with (linear) views of time held by many Christians and Jews.

Ideas for plenaries

1. Use the Reflection from the *Student Book*.
2. Ask students to volunteer to explain cyclical time and linear time using either:
    - the smart/whiteboard
    - a rap or rhyme that they have written
    - a physical demonstration.
3. Physically demonstrate cyclical and linear time with the whole class.
    - Arrange one group of students in the infinity symbol (or just a circle) and have them keep walking the loop.
    - Arrange another group in a straight line, with the first person raising their hands up, followed in turn by the rest until everyone has their hands up. Then they all put their hands down at same time to indicate the end of time.

Further class and homework activities

1. Ask students to rework the account of creation in Upanishads Audio Clip (text available in 1.4 Audio Handout) in a way that is suitable for young children, e.g. as a poem or song, or as a cartoon strip.
2. Play students 1.4 Upanishads Audio Clip before asking them to complete their own creation accounts, as a way of inspiring creativity.
3. 1.4 Cyclical or Linear Interactive Activity on the *Hinduism OxBox Online*.
4. 1.4 Creation Worksheet on the *Hinduism OxBox Online.*
5. Use 1.4 Starter Film Clips A and B on the *Hinduism OxBox Online* to supplement the Starter activity in the *Student Book*.
6. Further suggestions on page 28 of this book.

1.5 Do You Know Your Place? The Caste System

The unit in brief

This unit explains and explores 'varna', the Hindu caste system. Students investigate how caste may link to the purpose of life for some Hindus, and reflect on viewpoints from case study families.

Key ideas

- The caste system and why it exists
- The relevance of the caste system amongst Hindus today
- Whether the caste system encourages prejudice, and whether it is human nature to be prejudiced against others

Useful Words

caste, guna, varna

Skills practised

- Numeracy: creating pie charts and allocating percentages
- Reflection: considering how students feel about the class system
- Reasoning: looking at different possible responses to the issue of caste and reaching informed conclusions

Resources

- 1.5 Caste Film Clip A: Nisha Patani talks about caste
- 1.5 Caste Film Clip B: Mrs Morris talks about the caste system and about Gandhi
- 1.5 Film Worksheet: students assess their understanding of the case study film clips by linking ideas to the *Student Book*
- 1.5 Lesson Player: a ready-to-go presentation with built-in resources and teacher notes
- 1.5 Varna Interactive Activity: students drag the name of each varna to its description
- 1 Image Gallery: a useful gallery of photos and film stills from the chapter
- 1.5 Self-Assessment Sheet: students evaluate their learning against the lesson objectives

Ideas for starters

1. Display a range of jobs/professions (say, ten different roles) and ask students to rate each one as 1, 2, or 3 – 1 being the most important to society and 3 the least important. They could go on to share the reasons for their ratings.

2 Explore the idea of class in the UK:

a) Use a range of images to depict class, ranging from the royal family to a homeless person.

b) Ask students to consider, having looked at the images, whether the class divide is still present today, and why.

c) Ask students what they think 'caste' might be.

Activity guidance

- For Activity 1, you could ask students to compare their diagrams and feed back as a class about how similar and/or different class and caste appear to be. You could draw out the idea that caste and class are both believed by many to be decided by birth. A key difference is that caste places priests and teachers of wisdom above the monarchy and government leaders.

Ideas for plenaries

1. Randomly allocate students with a letter (A, B, C, D) and move them to different parts of the room.
   - 'A's have to copy out some boring text in silence.
   - 'B's get to colour in a picture, but still in silence.
   - 'C's have a range of games to play or magazines to read, but may not speak.
   - 'D's can do whatever they want (within reason!).

   Ask students to reflect upon how they feel in the role and why. You should find that those in group A, for example, feel resentful of the freedom that has been given to group D. Link these impressions to the idea of the Hindu caste system. Might some Hindus feel restricted if their caste dictates their job?
2. Ask students to find out more about Mahatma Gandhi. They could create a fact-file, a 'Did you Know?' poster, or pretend to interview him as a way of considering his beliefs.
3. Extend students' understanding of caste prejudice by asking them to research Dalits (untouchables) in India. Otherwise known as the 'fifth caste', Dalits are still discriminated against in spite of legislation.

Further class and homework activities

1. Use 1.5 Varna Interactive Activity from the *Hinduism OxBox Online*.
   a) Ask students to link names of varna with their descriptions.
   b) Follow this up with a game. Give groups of students a soft ball, which is passed to the next person only after the person holding the ball names and translates one of the Hindu castes, or one of the Useful Words from the unit. Set a timer to ring so that students have to be as quick as possible to avoid being left 'holding the ball'.
2. 1.5 Caste Film Clips A and B on the *Hinduism OxBox Online*.
3. Use 1.5 Film Worksheet to assess student understanding of the case studies.
4. Further suggestions on page 28 of this book.

1.6 Do all Paths Lead to the Divine?

The unit in brief

This unit looks at the meaning of truth, including some truth claims, and examines some ways in which Hindu families share their faith.

Key ideas

- An exploration of the meaning and reality of truth
- What different faiths say 'truth' is in comparison to Hinduism
- Whether or not Gandhi's belief that all paths lead to God is true

Useful Words

atheist, pluralism, theist

Skills practised

- Interpretation: looking at quotations and analysing possible meanings
- Literacy: producing a lively article
- Teamwork: working with others in a range of group tasks
- Enquiry: asking questions about what truth is and whether we can know it

Resources

- 1.6 Beliefs Film Clip A: Miran talks about faith issues
- 1.6 Beliefs Film Clip B: Nisha and Nirav Patani talk about faith issues
- 1.6 Faiths Interactive Activity: students match images of different people to their faith
- 1.6 Film Worksheet: students assess their understanding of the case study film clips by linking ideas to the *Student Book*
- 1.6 Lesson Player: a ready-to-go presentation with built-in resources and teacher notes
- 1 Image Gallery: a useful gallery of photos and film stills from the chapter
- 1.6 Self-Assessment Sheet: students evaluate their learning against the lesson objectives

Ideas for starters

1. Use the starter from the *Student Book*.
2. Present a range of statements and ask students to decide whether they are fact or belief. For example, 'Angels exist', 'There are seven days in a week', 'Murder is wrong', 'Some people become ghosts when they die', 'London hosted the Olympic and Paralympic Games in 2012'.
3. Present images of people from different faiths and ask: 'What do they have in common? What might they disagree about?'
4. Present copies of the Bible, the Qur'an, any Hindu sacred text, the Guru Granth Sahib, the Pali Canon, the Torah and any

other sacred texts you can access, or images of the above. Ask students: 'Do they all contain truth? What about? Is one more true than others? Is the oldest/youngest/longest/shortest more or less likely to be true? Why or why not?'

Activity guidance

- Activity 1 asks students to consider whether 'All paths lead to the Divine' includes atheism. This is a good opportunity to cover a more secular world view and explore the idea that atheism could also be considered to be a belief system and not just the absence of belief.
- Activity 4, which asks students to research the key beliefs of different faith systems, could be fed back to the class. For more in-depth comparisons, you could use the following units from other books in the series: Unit 1.1 in the *Christianity Student Book*, or 5.6 in the *Islam Student Book*.

Ideas for plenaries

1. Use the Reflection from the *Student Book*. This question would also work well in the context of a class debate.
2. Ask students to create a visual summary of the theory that 'All paths lead to the Divine'. Ask them to include quotations from case studies, religious scripture and religious leaders. They could find a visual way of showing different 'strands' of one thing (for example, paths up a mountain, a maypole, streams into a river).
3. Ask students to vote for which of Gandhi's teachings is the most interesting and ask them to explain why.
4. Ask students to work in pairs and find evidence from other Hindu teachings to support Gandhi's views.

Further class and homework activities

1. 1.6 Faiths Interactive Activity on the *Hinduism OxBox Online* would work well as an alternative starter activity for this unit. You could ask students to find out more about the figures featured in the activity and why they believe what they do. This could be extended by asking students to research other famous followers of a range of faiths or belief systems.
2. 1.6 Beliefs Film Clips A and B on the *Hinduism OxBox Online*.
3. 1.6 Film Worksheet on the *Hinduism OxBox Online*.
4. Further suggestions on page 28 of this book.

Chapter 1 Further Suggestions

These suggestions are addressed directly to students.

1.1 Namaste! What is the Divine?

1. What do we really mean by 'respect'? Share your reflections as a blog, poem, or piece of art. ***
2. Investigate other forms of greetings from a range of faiths and cultures. */**/***
3. Choose one greeting and explore its meaning(s), history and uses in detail (Who uses this greeting? When? Where? How?). **/***

1.2 One Supreme Spirit in Many Forms

1. Create a collage or series of images (digital or printed) that reflects ways in which people may see 'the Divine in Nature'. You can use cut-out pictures or photographs you have taken. *
2. Design a deity. As well as visual aspects, explain what qualities and features would appeal to you or others. **
3. Investigate amazing aspects of nature. Are these amazing things proof of some kind of creator, or just how things happen to be? Many Hindus consider evolution itself to be part of the plan, but for some others the question remains: designed or accidental? ***
4. Investigate a range of belief systems (current and historical) and make a mind-map or chart that lists some monotheistic, polytheistic, pantheistic and atheist ideas. **/***

1.3 Where are We Going? The Cycle of Life (and Death)

1. Explore accounts about reincarnation from around the world and evaluate how believable they are. */**/***
2. Creative homework: If you could be any living creature at all, what would you choose and why? *
3. Investigate some beliefs about death from an ancient faith or culture (e.g. Egyptian, Aztec, Druid, Greek, Roman, Viking). Compare and contrast your findings with: (**a**) your own views; and (**b**) Hindu beliefs about reincarnation. **/***
4. Some people believe that child geniuses, like the composer Mozart, are proof of reincarnation. They claim that the only way in which someone can be so talented at such a young age, is because they were born 'knowing' or 'carrying' those talents from a past life. Do you agree? Investigate this theory further and present your own views as a 'news report', blog, or mini-documentary. ***

1.4 Where are We? Time and Place

1. Find three different creation stories or theories from different belief systems (including one non-religious). Identify what they have in common, and what they differ on. Which is the most convincing and why? ***
2. Consider the concept from *The Hitch Hiker's Guide to the Galaxy* that 'aliens' created Earth (as a building project!). Is this any more or less believable or unbelievable than the idea that God/ the Divine created us? */**/***

1.5 Do You Know Your Place? The Caste System

1. In the past (and still today, sometimes) the caste and class systems often decided how much power people had and how much respect they were given by others. Hold a class debate or reflection exercise: 'What's more important – respect or power?' Use examples and reasoning skills to support your view. */**/***
2. Use words, pictures and diagrams to answer the question 'Is everybody born equal?' */**/***
3. Homework: Reflect and discuss (with friends and family) the questions, 'Is there any belief or cause that you would be willing to suffer beatings for, to go to prison for, and even to die for, in the way that Gandhi suffered and gave his life to *ahimsa* and equality? What is it and why?'; or 'Why do you think there isn't anything that feels important enough to make that kind of sacrifice for?' */**/***

1.6 Do all Paths Lead to the Divine?

1. Challenge! How many different religions can you find the names of?
   Step 1 (in class): List all that you can without any research.

   Step 2 (homework): Add to your list, in your own words, by researching. */**/***
2. Investigate and construct a fact-file for a religion you hadn't ever heard of before. (You could ask your teacher for a list of religions to choose from, or this task could follow on from Activity 1 above.) */**/***
3. Compare the fact-files from Activity 2 above. Do the religions investigated have more in common or more that's different? Do the findings suggest that 'All paths *do* or *do not* lead to the Divine'? */**/***

Chapter 1 Assessment

Assessment in the *Student Book*

You will find an assessment task at the end of every chapter which focuses on AT2. In this chapter, the task asks students to explore, evaluate and reflect on the purpose of life, both from a Hindu perspective and their own point of view.

In the *Student Book* (and on the supporting worksheets), you'll find guidance about levels of assessment that you can use to help your students understand what their work should include. You could ask them to use these criteria for self- or peer-assessment once they've completed the task.

Living Faiths Assessment

Student Book
- Assessment Task
- Levels Guidance

OxBox Online
- Auto-Marked Test
- Assessment Task Presentation
- Assessment Worksheets

Assessment Task for Chapter 1 (pages **20–21** of the *Hinduism Student Book*)

Objectives
- Explore and evaluate some key Hindu beliefs about the purpose of life
- Reflect on the meaning of life and justify an argument
- Develop effective presentation skills

Task
Use a range of presentation techniques to share your answers to the questions:
- What is the meaning of life, according to a Hindu?
- Do you agree or disagree with the Hindu view?

You must include reference to some Hindu ideas about the purpose of life, the Divine and atman.

Assessment in *OxBox Online*

On the *Hinduism OxBox Online*, you'll find resources to use when introducing the assessment task to the class.

You can use the *Chapter 1 Assessment Task Presentation* as a front-of-class tool to help your students unpack the assessment criteria, and understand what is expected of them.

Chapter 1 Assessment Worksheets accompany the task, so that once you finish the presentation, your students can easily get started.

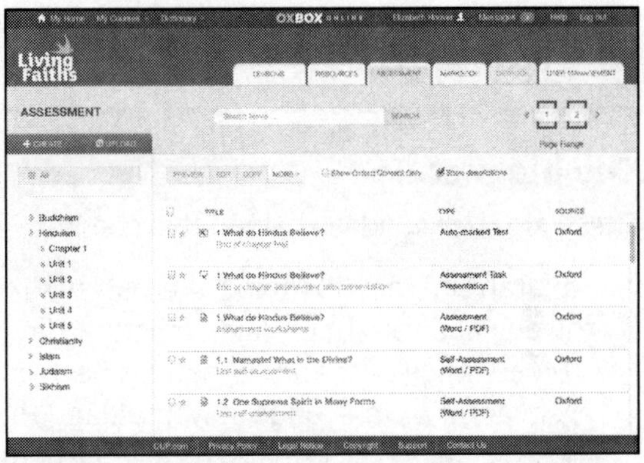

▲ Assessment resources for Chapter 1 on the *Hinduism Oxbox Online*

Auto-marked tests

The *Hinduism OxBox Online* also contains auto-marked tests for each chapter to help save you time setting questions and marking for AT1. The test for this chapter 15 contains questions and will take most students about half an hour. Test results are automatically stored in the markbook.

Digital markbook

A markbook and a reporting function complete the *OxBox Online* assessment package, so you can keep all your students' test results and assessment scores in one place. This can include the auto-marked tests as well as pieces of work you or the students have marked by hand.

Chapter 2 Overview
Where do Hindu Beliefs Come From?

Helping you deliver Key Stage 3 RE

This chapter addresses the following areas of the Programme of Study:

Key concepts

Beliefs, teachings and sources

- Interpret teachings, sources, authorities and ways of life (including the history of Hinduism) in order to understand religions and beliefs

Key processes

Learning about religion

- Investigate the impact of religious beliefs and teachings on individuals and communities
- Interpret a range of sources, texts, authorities, and forms of religious and spiritual expression from a variety of contexts

Learning from religion

- Reflect on the relationship between beliefs and teachings

The big picture

These are the key ideas behind this chapter:

- Sanatan Dharma (meaning 'eternal laws') refers to the age and variety of Hindu practice. Hinduism has a broad range of scripture that has been compiled over centuries in a range of ways. Many Hindus read these sacred texts, but also receive wisdom from gurus (spiritual teachers/life coaches).
- Hindu culture is extremely varied. It has its origins in India, but it also has millions of believers worldwide. There are difficulties when translating texts from the original Sanskrit into a wide range of regional and global languages *and* different interpretations of sacred writing exist.
- The Hindu priest has important roles in worship and daily life. Hinduism does not have one specific leader or sacred text, which is its key difference from some other faiths.

Chapter outline

Use this to give students a mental road map of the chapter:

2.1 Ancient Symbols of Hinduism – introduces the Hindu symbols of the swastika and the Aum, and explains the origins of Hinduism

2.2 So Much Scripture! – explains the type and range of Hindu sacred texts, and includes the use of case studies

2.3 What does it Mean? Intelligent Interpretation – explains how language, personality and culture may affect the understanding and use of sacred texts, and includes the use of case studies

2.4 Who Guides the Way? Guidance from Gurus – introduces the concept of gurus and gives some modern examples

2.5 Who's in Charge? No One? – explains that Hinduism has no single leader and introduces the role of the Hindu priest

Opportunities for assessment

Summative assessments on the *Hinduism OxBox Online* include auto-marked tests, interactive activities, and self-assessment worksheets.

The end-of-chapter assessment task in the *Student Book* provides formative assessment. Supporting materials for the assessment task can be found on the *Hinduism OxBox Online*, such as the Assessment Task Presentation and the related worksheets.

There are other opportunities for assessment too. For example, you could use some of the activities or reflection points throughout each *Student Book* unit, or some of the 'Further Suggestions' at the end of this chapter.

Getting ready for this chapter

- Find some Hindu sacred texts for students to see and handle, such as the Bhagavad Gita.
- Familiarize yourself with some of the teachings of the gurus in Unit 2.4, so that you can encourage in-depth discussion.

Objectives and outcomes for this chapter

Objectives	Unit	Outcomes
Most students will:		Most students will be able to:
• learn about the origins of Hinduism • investigate and analyse how symbols may be misinterpreted • reflect on the idea that the meaning of symbols may change over time.	**2.1**	• describe and explain some of the origins of Hinduism • explain the meanings of the swastika and Aum symbols • discuss how the swastika has been interpreted differently in recent history.
• recognize the diversity of sacred writing in Hinduism • investigate some examples of scripture in Hinduism • evaluate the relevance of ancient teachings to the modern world.	**2.2**	• explain why there are so many sacred texts and name some of them • identify which texts are smriti and shruti and the differences between them • Express personal views about the relevance of Hindu scripture in the modern world and be able to see both sides of the argument.
• learn that there are a number of languages associated with Hinduism • evaluate whether meaning may be 'lost in translation' • develop an understanding of how it feels to learn new languages.	**2.3**	• explain the origins of the written Hindu texts and describe the various translations that exist today • understand the problems involved in translating material accurately • consider the work involved for young people who learn a different script as part of their faith/culture.
• identify some qualities of a good spiritual leader • investigate and evaluate the role and influence of gurus in the lives of some Hindus • reflect on the qualities a guru should possess.	**2.4**	• identify the characteristics and qualities of effective and/or attractive spiritual leaders • explain the popularity of certain named gurus for some Hindus today • explain what they think makes a good guru or mata.
• explain some reasons why Hinduism does not have one set of rules or one leader • explore the role of a Hindu priest • reflect on how religious leaders can inspire people to follow them.	**2.5**	• explain how individual Hindus follow their own set of rules, based on a variety of sources • describe and explain some of the duties and functions of a Hindu priest • analyse the power of religious leaders to inspire.

2.1 Ancient Symbols of Hinduism

The unit in brief

This unit covers some of the history and evolution of Hinduism, beginning with an exploration of the swastika and its different uses. It also explains the Aum symbol.

Key ideas

- The history and meaning of the swastika and Aum symbols
- The concept of Sanatan Dharma
- The evolution of Hinduism

Useful Words

Aum, Aryan, prejudice, Sanatan Dharma, swastika

Skills practised

- Information analysis: exploring and evaluating the history of the swastika
- Communication: sharing understanding and evaluations

Resources

- 2.1 History Interactive Activity: students fill the gaps to assess their understanding of the unit
- 2.1 Symbols Worksheet: students annotate key Hindu symbols with their meanings and associations
- 2.1 Chanting Audio Clip: a chant which demonstrates the different sounds of the Aum
- 2 Image Gallery: a useful gallery of photos and film stills from the chapter
- 2.1 Lesson Player: a ready-to-go presentation with built-in resources and teacher notes
- 2.1 Self-Assessment Sheet: students evaluate their learning against the lesson objectives

Ideas for starters

1. Use the starter from the *Student Book*. You could also show historical video clips of Nazi Germany, e.g. 'the road to legal persecution' from the BBC's Learning Zone website.
2. Present students with, or facilitate their investigation of, a range of responses to the question 'How old is Hinduism?' Different sites/books give differing figures. Use this as a platform for their investigations into the history of Hinduism in this unit.
3. Ask students to think about and discuss why Hinduism is called Hinduism. Connect to 'Buddhism' from Buddha and 'Christianity' from Christ – where does the 'Hindu' bit come from?
4. Present the two symbols from this unit and ask whether students can guess what they might symbolize.
5. Ask students to draw and/or write any symbols that they associate with Hinduism and say what they think they mean.

Activity guidance

You may wish to develop the comparison between different faith symbols by using Unit 1.5 in the *Buddhism Student Book*, Chapter 3 in the *Sikhism Student Book*, or Unit 3.1 in the *Christianity Student Book*. You may also want to investigate BBC Learning Zone's online clips on the Nazi Party and persecution.

Ideas for plenaries

1. Use the Reflection from the *Student Book*, and ask students to share and compare their responses.
2. Set a research task/project into the history of the swastika, and/or different cultures that have used it, and/or different meanings associated with it.
3. Ask students to investigate and present a timeline of faiths. This could be a class display, with pairs tackling different religions, or an individual task. Ask them to include major philosophical, social and scientific movements, as well as religions. This will help students develop a broader perspective as well as enabling them to 'place' Hinduism in history.
4. Ask students to choose one of the quotations from Hindu sacred texts about the Aum. Ask them to:
   a) rewrite the quotation in their own words
   b) write down anything that confuses them about it
   c) discuss their questions with a partner
   d) feed back to the class.
   You may wish to play 2.1 Chanting Audio Clip to help them better understand the use of the Aum.
5. Set a research task into other Hindu symbols and their meanings i.e. the lotus or Yantra. Students could focus on one in detail or investigate a range of symbols.

Further class and homework activities

1. Use 2.1 History Interactive Activity on the *Hinduism OxBox Online* as a plenary for this unit.
2. Students should learn the Useful Words and definitions explored in this *Student Book* unit for a quick quiz next lesson.
3. Use the images of the two symbols from 2 Image Gallery on the *Hinduism OxBox Online* either to support a starter asking students what the symbols might mean, or to support the Reflection in the *Student Book*.
4. 2.1 Timeline Worksheet on the *Hinduism OxBox Online*.
5. Further suggestions on page 42 of this book.

2.2 So Much Scripture!

The unit in brief

This unit looks at the diversity of scripture in Hinduism, including the names of key texts, and includes case studies of young Hindus explaining the reasons for their personal favourites.

Key ideas

- The diversity of sacred writing in Hinduism
- Where the scriptures originate from in Hinduism
- How relevant ancient teachings are to modern Hindus

Useful Words

moral, sacred texts, scripture, shruti, smriti

Skills practised

- Interpretation: evaluating sacred texts and teachings in a book review
- Investigation: considering the validity of some sacred texts
- Communication: using creativity to re-tell a story from Hindu scripture
- Personal reflection: thinking about the personal impact that texts (religious or otherwise) have had
- Cross-curricular: using literacy skills to analyse texts and communicate understanding and views

Resources

- 2.2 Stories Film Clip A: Neha and Nirav Dave relate the story of Divali
- 2.2 Stories Film Clip B: Nisha and Nirav Patani tell a story about baby Krishna.
- 2.2 Film Worksheet: students assess their understanding of the case study film clips by linking ideas to the *Student Book*
- 2.2 Lesson Player: a ready-to-go presentation with built-in resources and teacher notes
- 2.2 Texts Interactive Activity: students drag the names of sacred texts to their descriptions
- 2 Image Gallery: a useful gallery of photos and film stills from the chapter
- 2.2 Self-Assessment Sheet: students evaluate their learning against the lesson objectives

Ideas for starters

1. Use the Starter in the *Student Book*.
2. Present a range of popular sound bites to the class (e.g. Voltaire on free speech, Gandhi's 'eye for an eye and the world will soon be blind', the first section of Martin Luther King's 'I have a dream' speech). In pairs or groups, ask students to analyse what makes these quotations have impact and longevity.

3. Present a list of Hindu sacred texts and ask 'What do these books have in common?', and/or present a range of influential writings, e.g. Darwin's *On the Origin of Species*, Stephen Hawking's *A Brief History of Time*, Einstein's *Relativity* and ask 'What do these books have in common?'. Highlight the fact that these texts have changed the way people view the world.

Activity guidance

- For the starter in the *Student Book*, you could ask students who are finding it difficult to think of examples to note down any quote or lyric which 'stays with them' (words they cannot forget), and then to reflect about what makes some words 'memorable'.
- For Activity **1**, you could split students into groups and ask them to share their thoughts – imagining that they are in a book club role-play. The activity could be extended further by asking students to design a suitable and eye-catching book cover to go with the blurb they have composed.

Ideas for plenaries

1. Use the Reflection from the *Student Book* and ask students to share and compare their thoughts.
2. Ask students to present their outcomes from Activity 2 to the class, or to each other in groups. This is a good opportunity for peer-assessment.
3. Ask students, in pairs or small groups, to investigate the origins and key features of different Hindu texts and present their findings in a fact-file. The class could collate the fact-files to create a 'Guide to Hindu scripture'.
4. Try to source actual or Internet copies of comics produced to engage young readers with accounts from scripture. Ask students to consider 'Is scripture as comic strips a useful and fun way to present religious texts, or not?'

Further class and homework activities

1. Use 2.2 Texts Interactive Activity from the *Hinduism OxBox Online*.
2. Students should learn the Useful Words and definitions explored in this *Student Book* unit for a quick quiz next lesson.
3. Watch 2.2 Stories Film Clips A and B on the *Hinduism OxBox Online*.
4. Use 2.2 Film Worksheet from the *Hinduism OxBox Online*.
5. As a homework, set students the challenge of creating acrostic poems for 'shruti' and 'smriti' to help them understand and remember what the terms mean.
6. Further suggestions on page 42 of this book.

2.3 What does it Mean? Intelligent Interpretation

The unit in brief

This unit explores issues related to language and faith. Students are encouraged to investigate whether the value of scripture 'changes' in translation or not. It includes a case study of a young Hindu girl who has extra schooling to learn Gujarati.

Key ideas

- The history of scripture and who wrote it down
- The range of languages associated with Hinduism
- Whether meaning may be 'lost in translation'

Useful Word

mantra

Skills practised

- Thinking: explaining how meaning changes with translation and sharing of information
- Empathy: understanding how 'extra' languages may be daunting and/or enriching for young believers
- Analysis: explaining whether the source or meaning of a text is the most important factor for believers and others

Resources

- 2.3 Gujarati Film Clip: Nisha Patani talks about Gujarati school
- 2.3 Film Worksheet: students assess their understanding of the case study film clips by linking ideas to the *Student Book*
- 2.3 Lesson Player: a ready-to-go presentation with built-in resources and teacher notes
- 2.3 Language Interactive Activity: students fill the gaps in a paragraph on language and sacred texts
- 2 Image Gallery: a useful gallery of photos and film stills from the chapter
- 2.3 Self-Assessment Sheet: students evaluate their learning against the lesson objectives

Ideas for starters

1. Use the starter from the *Student Book*. Beforehand, provide a message and get students to play Chinese Whispers – with the message travelling two ways around the room.
2. Play an alternative written version of Chinese Whispers, by providing a written message that the first student in the circle has to re-write in their own words. Fold over the original version before passing it on to the next person. This could travel two ways around the room.

3. Present a simple phrase such as 'hello' or 'welcome' in a range of languages and ask students to identify what the words have in common.
4. Ask students to think about or list the languages they speak/read/write/can understand/can speak a few words of.

Activity guidance

You could follow up Activity **2** by asking students to 'send' their social networking posts on paper, or by speaking, and to comment on each other's posts.

Ideas for plenaries

1. Use the Reflection from the *Student Book*, asking students to share and compare their responses.
2. Ask students how many words they can think of with more than one meaning. Ask them to write a sketch in which there is confusion (or comedy) caused by people interpreting some words in different ways.
3. Show or use a phrase in sign language and ask students if it looks exactly the same as the word it's showing. Ask 'How can we know?'
4. Search online for examples of amusing mistranslations, e.g. road signs or subtitles. Ask students how great an effect the mistakes have. Follow this up by asking 'Could there be some cases in scripture where a key word has been mistranslated in the past? How might this affect beliefs and lives?'.
5. Explain to students that how people interpret texts can have a big impact on how they live. You could provide the example that some Christians understand 'dominion' over the world (in the Book of Genesis from the Bible) to mean that they are stewards who have the responsibility of taking care of the Earth and other creatures, whereas others interpret 'dominion' to mean 'masters' who can do what they want with the Earth and other creatures. Ask students to role-play a conversation between two Christians with different interpretations and a pantheistic Hindu (see Unit 1.1), which illustrates their different beliefs and interpretations.

Further class and homework activities

1. Students should learn the Useful Words and definitions explored in this *Student Book* unit for a quick quiz next lesson.
2. 2.3 Language Interactive Activity on the *Hinduism OxBox Online* would work well as a plenary activity.
3. 2.3 Gujarati Film Clip on the *Hinduism OxBox Online.*
4. 2.3 Film Worksheet on the *Hinduism OxBox Online.*
5. Further suggestions on page 42 of this book.

2.4 Who Guides the Way? Guidance from Gurus

The unit in brief

This unit explores the history and roles of gurus and mata, and explains what 'guru' really means. The evolution of these roles is described and modern practice evaluated by considering the work and influence of two figures who are currently popular.

Key ideas

- What makes a good spiritual leader
- The role and influence of gurus and mata in the lives of some Hindus
- The teachings and popularity of a guru and a mata

Useful Words

ashrama, disciple, guru, mata, swami

Skills practised

- Interpretation: understanding quotations by influential Hindus
- Thinking: exploring a range of factors that influence a guru or mata's appeal
- Reflection: considering charismatic qualities and human nature
- Evaluation: analysing different messages and characteristics
- Debate: using thinking and communication skills

Resources

- 2.4 Gurus Interactive Activity: students must link key terms and people to the correct description
- 2.4 Quotations Worksheet: students must rewrite some gurus' teachings in their own words
- 2 Image Gallery: a useful gallery of photos and film stills from the chapter
- 2.4 Lesson Player: a ready-to-go presentation with built-in resources and teacher notes
- 2.4 Self-Assessment Sheet: students evaluate their learning against the lesson objectives

Ideas for starters

1. Use the starter from the *Student Book*. Feed back as a class.
2. Show students a poster from the 2002 film *The Guru* and ask them what impression it gives them of what a guru is. How accurate do they think it is?
3. Ask students to discuss in small groups who they look up to and why.
4. Group, Pair, Solo (discuss, list, write a sentence): what makes someone a good role model?

Activity guidance

You could ask students to explore various guru websites (where many gurus/ mata choose to publish their wisdom and teachings). However, remember to check the content of websites first.

Ideas for plenaries

1. Use the Reflection from the *Student Book*. You could share and compare responses.
2. Conduct a timed activity in threes. The first person has to name a new word from the *Student Book*, the second person explains it and the third person adds to the explanation or gives an example. The aim is to get through all the new words in the time allowed.
3. Ask students to choose either the guru or the mata from this unit as a case study. They have to find out more about them and create a fact-file.
4. Conduct a timed activity in pairs or small groups. Provide copies of up to four quotes from the *Student Book*. The first person has to explain the quotes and the next has to add to the explanation or give another related quote/teaching from a guru or mata. The aim is to get through all the quotes in the time allowed.

Further class and homework activities

1. As a homework activity, students could write three 'wise sayings' that they would put on their website if they were a guru or mata and present them artistically.
2. Ask students to think about what make a Great Guru or Marvellous Mata and create a list or spider diagram of qualities and characteristics.
3. 2.4 Gurus Interactive Activity on the *Hinduism OxBox Online* would work well as a plenary.
4. 2.4 Quotations Worksheet on the *Hinduism OxBox Online.*
5. Further suggestions on page 42 of this book.

2.5 Who's in Charge? No One?

The unit in brief

This unit considers why there is no founder or one leader in Hinduism, and compares this situation with other faiths. Students explore how Hindus establish 'rules for life', and also consider the role of the Hindu priest.

Key ideas

- Unlike most other faiths, Hinduism has no founder nor one particular leader
- A Hindu might follow their own particular set of rules based on, for example, family tradition and wisdom from gurus
- The Hindu priest's role in the life of Hindus

Useful Words

mandir, religious founder, ritual

Skills practised

- Reflection: considering what role a new religious leader might play in today's world
- Reasoning: deciding what the most important duties of a Hindu priest are
- Communication: considering the possibility of women as Hindu leaders

Resources

- 2.5 Rules Interactive Activity: students must identify the possible sources of religious guidance for Hindus
- 2.5 Priest Worksheet: students categorize some of the duties that a Hindu priest carries out
- 2 Image Gallery: a useful gallery of photos and film stills from the chapter
- 2.5 Lesson Player: a ready-to-go presentation with built-in resources and teacher notes
- 2.5 Self-Assessment Sheet: students evaluate their learning against the lesson objectives

Ideas for starters

1. Use the starter from the *Student Book*.
2. See how many faiths students can name, and then ask them the question 'Who's in charge?'. See if they can name any other key religious leaders too.
3. Ask students to share in groups, and present on a big sheet, what they think makes a good religious leader. Feed back as a class, asking students to give reasons for their answers.

Ideas for plenaries

1. Use the Reflection from the *Student Book*.
2. Use students' responses to Activity **4** in the *Student Book* to stage a class debate.
3. If possible, you could arrange for students to visit a local mandir and/or invite a Hindu priest to speak to the class about their work.
4. Play a timed 'Pass the ball' game in groups (the aim is not to be holding the ball when the buzzer/bell goes off). Students should take it in turns to name one of the ways in which a Hindu might decide how to make decisions about their own faith rules (for example, guidance from scripture, gurus, their own conscience, etc.) for a set amount of time before a buzzer/bell goes off.

Further class and homework activities

1. Use 2.5 Rules Interactive Activity on the *Hinduism OxBox Online* as a starter or plenary.
2. 2.5 Priest Worksheet on the *Hinduism OxBox Online.*
3. Students should learn the Useful Words and definitions explored in this *Student Book* unit for a quick quiz next lesson.
4. Further suggestions on page 42 of this book.

Chapter 2 Further Suggestions

These suggestions are addressed directly to students.

2.1 Ancient Symbols of Hinduism

1 Apart from the swastika, the other main symbol associated with Hinduism is the Aum. Investigate what the Aum signifies and ways in which it is used. */**/***

2 Design a poster that provides detailed information about the Aum. **/***

3 Investigate the history of how Hinduism developed and use map skills from Geography to mark some important places on a map of India, including the Indus Valley and the River Ganges. */**/***

4 Does the lack of a founder and a single sacred text make Hindu philosophy more or less true than faiths with a clear foundation and scripture? **/***

2.2 So Much Scripture!

1 Investigate some stories about Lord Krishna. Choose one that really appeals to you and use it as the basis of an article or presentation to the class, where you explain the message in the story as well as presenting it creatively. ***

2 The Ramayana was chosen by Neha and Nirav Dave as their favourite text because it includes the 'story of Divali'. Investigate this popular story and make a list of the key characters. */**

3 Create a mind-map of the key figures in the story of Divali and the qualities (e.g. loyalty) associated with them. Also include the themes and symbols in the story. Use shape and colour to show connections and differences. ***

4 At Divali, the story is re-told in many different ways, including drama and dance. Plan and script or choreograph a Divali presentation of the story. */**/***

2.3 What does it Mean? Intelligent Interpretation

1 Find the words of the Gayatri Mantra online. Re-write them in 'student speak' to show your understanding of the message. */**/***

2 In pairs or small groups, compare and contrast your 'translation' of the Gayatri Mantra. What reasons could there be for differences in interpretation? **/***

3 Try to translate some favourite words or lyrics (explored in the starter activity in Unit 2.2 of the *Student Book*) into another language you have some knowledge of – either from school or home. How difficult is it? Are there any different ways in which you could have translated them? ***

2.4 Who Guides the Way? Guidance from Gurus

1 Many popular gurus and mata have charisma that makes people believe what they say and want to follow them. List all of the people you can think of (living or dead) who have or had charisma. */**

2 Choose one person from Activity **1** above to investigate in detail and produce a fact-file, information booklet or poster about them. Make sure you include evidence about what makes them charismatic! **/***

3 Sikhism is based on the teachings of ten gurus – the first of whom, Guru Nanak, was from a Hindu family. Explore some of Guru Nanak's key teachings and assess how different or similar they are to Hindu teachings. **/***

4 The Buddha, like Guru Nanak (Activity 3 above), was also brought up in a Hindu family. Investigate the life story and main beliefs of Buddha (including his original name). Present your findings as a detailed fact-file, and assess how different or similar his teachings are to Hindu teachings. ***

2.5 Who's in Charge? No One?

1 Create your own 'Hindu priest' website, showing their roles and duties. Include an introduction and 'news' section, plus links to different aspects of the role (e.g. marriage ceremonies, blessing new homes). */**/***

2 Research the titles given to religious leaders (like maharaj in Hinduism) of as many different belief systems as you can. Present them as a list and include pictures. */**/***

3 Find out the names of some key leaders from belief systems around the world or in Britain and present your findings as a poster, PowerPoint presentation, or booklet that (ideally) includes pictures and some extra information about each person. **/***

4 The Queen has a unique position as both Head of State and Head of The Church of England. She has promised to be 'Defender of *the* Faith' but Prince Charles has publically stated that he would prefer to be 'Defender of *Faiths*' to show respect and acknowledge that Britain today is a nation of many different belief systems. Draw up a 'pros' and 'cons' list of why the monarch should or should not change the oath to defend faith. Then create a social networking post that sums up your final decision and the reasons for it.

Chapter 2 Assessment

Assessment in the *Student Book*

You will find an assessment task at the end of every chapter which focuses on AT2. In this chapter, the task asks students to draw on their learning about Hindu teachings to debate the idea that 'the pen is mightier than the sword'.

In the *Student Book* (and on the supporting worksheets), you'll find guidance about levels of assessment that you can use to help your students understand what their work should include. You could ask them to use these criteria for self- or peer-assessment once they've completed the task.

> **Living Faiths Assessment**
>
> ***Student Book***
> - Assessment Task
> - Levels Guidance
>
> ***OxBox Online***
> - Auto-Marked Test
> - Assessment Task Presentation
> - Assessment Worksheets

Assessment Task for Chapter 2 (pages **32–33** of the *Hinduism Student Book*)

Objectives

- Interpret and apply quotes from Hindu sacred texts and philosophers or Hindu leaders
- Develop and communicate your own point of view
- Evaluate evidence from a debate and make informed conclusions

Task

Draw on your learning about Hindu scriptures to debate the statement: 'the pen is mightier than the sword'. Do you agree or disagree, in light of your work on Hinduism? Explain your reasons.

a) Prepare: In groups of four or five, identify and prepare quotes and examples to support each side of the argument.

b) Debate: Use your identified ideas to support what you say in a class debate about this issue.

c) Summarize: Use your preparation and ideas put forward during the debate to help you to produce a written (and visual if you wish) summary of the debate, including the pros and cons, and then your own judgment on which side is most convincing.

Assessment in *OxBox Online*

On the *Hinduism OxBox Online*, you'll find resources to use when introducing the assessment task to the class.

You can use the *Chapter 2 Assessment Task Presentation* as a front-of-class tool to help your students unpack the assessment criteria, and understand what is expected of them.

Chapter 2 Assessment Worksheets accompany the task, so that once you finish the presentation, your students can easily get started.

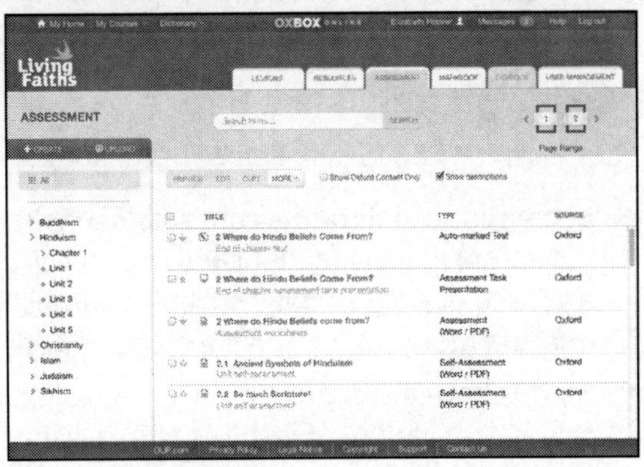

▲ Assessment resources for Chapter 2 on the *Hinduism Oxbox Online*

Auto-marked tests

The *Hinduism OxBox Online* also contains auto-marked tests for each chapter to help save you time setting questions and marking for AT1. The test for this chapter contains 15 questions and will take most students about half an hour. Test results are automatically stored in the markbook.

Digital markbook

A markbook and a reporting function complete the OxBox Online assessment package, so you can keep all your students' test results and assessment scores in one place. This can include the auto-marked tests as well as pieces of work you or the students have marked by hand.

Chapter 3 Overview
Belonging to the Hindu Faith

Helping you deliver Key Stage 3 RE

This chapter addresses the following areas of the Programme of Study:

Key concepts

Practices and ways of life

- Explore the impact of religions and beliefs on how people live their lives

Expressing meaning

- Appreciate that individuals and cultures express their beliefs and values through many different forms

Key processes

Learning about religion

- Investigate the impact of religious beliefs and teachings on individuals, communities and societies, the reasons for commitment and the causes of diversity
- Explain religious beliefs, practices and commitments, including their transmission by people, texts and traditions

Learning from religion

- Express insights into the significance and value of religion and other worldviews for human relationships personally, locally and globally

The big picture

These are the key ideas behind this chapter:

- Some Hindus follow the concepts of bhakti (devotion), karma (action) and gnaan (wisdom) in a variety of ways. A key concept is varnashrama dharma (duties based on life stage and caste).
- Hindus have a variety of rituals (e.g. puja) and celebrate a variety of festivals (e.g. Raksha Bandhan).
- Hindus may demonstrate and share their spirituality through worship at home and at the mandir (temple). They perform rituals as well as expressing their spirituality through life choices, the arts and architecture.

Chapter outline

Use this to give students a mental road map of the chapter:

3.1 Karma: A Sense of Purpose – applies learning about karma and karmic debt to situations in life, and also introduces the concept of ahimsa

3.2 A Rough Guide to Festivals and Rituals – uses family case studies to introduce several Hindu festivals

3.3 Special Feature: A Family Affair – uses case studies to introduce Hindu ideas about family life and interaction

3.4 Love, Love, Love! Expressing Faith – investigates three of the most popular ways in which many Hindus express their love for the Divine (bhakti, karma and gnaan)

3.5 What's My Role? Hindu Life Stages – analyses the concept of varnashrama dharma and uses case studies to investigate its relevance to modern Hinduism

3.6 Wonderful Ways to Worship: Yoga, Dance and Songs – uses case studies to help explain how Hindus connect to the Divine

Opportunities for assessment

Summative assessments on the *Hinduism OxBox Online* include auto-marked tests, interactive activities, and self-assessment worksheets.

The end-of-chapter assessment task in the *Student Book* provides formative assessment. Supporting materials for the assessment task can be found on the *Hinduism OxBox Online*, such as the Assessment Task Presentation and the related worksheets.

There are other opportunities for assessment too. For example, you could use some of the activities or reflection points throughout each *Student Book* unit, or some of the 'Further Suggestions' at the end of this chapter.

Getting ready for this chapter

- Visit a mandir or someone's home shrine to really experience it first hand. Watch 3.6 Worship Film Clip C if you have the *Hinduism OxBox Online* for a virtual tour of a mandir.

- It really is OK to make a shrine or perform puja in the classroom, as long as the intention is to educate. Hindu parents (or brave students) may be willing to share their own practice.
- It's worth practising some meditation or yoga alone at home before encouraging students to participate in it – the more comfortable you are, the better the learning experience. Alternatively, arrange for a practitioner to come in to take a special lesson.

Objectives and outcomes for this chapter

Objectives	Unit	Outcomes
Most students will:		Most students will be able to:
• develop understanding about the concept of karma • analyse the causes and purpose of suffering • evaluate the purpose of Mahatma Gandhi's life • consider what the purpose of their own life might be.	**3.1**	• explain the concept of karma • evaluate the concept of karmic debt and give examples of 'good' and 'bad' karma • identify ways in which Mahatma Gandhi changed his own life and the lives of others • express and evaluate their own purpose in life.
• identify and describe some popular Hindu festivals and rituals • understand and explain the purpose of ritual in faiths • explore why all humans seem to have rituals.	**3.2**	• name at least three Hindu festivals or rituals • explain the reasons behind some Hindu practice • give reasons why some humans have 'rituals' that are important to them.
• recognize the importance of family in Hinduism • learn that, for Hindus, participating in faith events is a way of learning • reflect on some Hindu beliefs about life and death.	**3.3**	• explain what an extended family is • identify ways in which some Hindus may learn more about Hinduism from their experience of faith events • express personal views about ways to commemorate the dead.
• reflect on the idea that 'love' has many meanings • investigate different ways in which Hindus show love for the Divine • identify some ways in which religious beliefs affect people's behaviour.	**3.4**	• use and understand the terms agape, eros, philos and storge • explain and give examples of bhakti, karma and gnaan • identify ways in which people's actions may be inspired by faith.
• develop an understanding of the Hindu belief in dharma (duty) • evaluate the value of having set goals and duties in life • reflect on their own place and role in the world.	**3.5**	• Be able to explain the concept of varnashrama dharma • give reasons for *and* against having certain duties in life decided by a person's faith • identify and evaluate their own goals or duties and reasons for them.
• identify the variety of ways in which Hindus may worship • reflect upon what it means to Hindus to connect with the Divine • identify and appreciate their own talents.	**3.6**	• identify a range of ways in which Hindus may worship • explain and give examples of their own understanding of 'connect with the Divine' • say 'I'm good at…' without feeling shy!

3.1 Karma: A Sense of Purpose!

The unit in brief

This unit explores the key concepts of karma, karmic debt and ahimsa (the principle of non-violence). Fate is examined through students' own experiences as a way in to karma, and there is reference to reincarnation (see Unit 1.3). Mahatma Gandhi is used as an example of someone who lived with purpose.

Key ideas

- The concepts of fate and karma
- How Mahatma Gandhi's life had purpose
- What the purpose of a student's own life might be

Useful Words

ahimsa, karma, karmic debt, spiritual fulfilment

Skills practised

- Self-awareness: engaging in spiritual reflection and taking the Ahimsa Challenge
- Applying learning: deciding what makes 'good' and bad' karma
- Communication: simplifying information and engaging in debate
- Reasoning: exploring multiple viewpoints and reaching informed conclusions

Resources

- 3.1 Karma Interactive Activity: students assess what counts as good, bad or neutral karma
- 3.1 Wealth and Fame Worksheet: students identify the positive and negative aspects of wealth and fame
- 3 Image Gallery: a useful gallery of photos and film stills from the chapter
- 3.1 Lesson Player: a ready-to-go presentation with built-in resources and teacher notes
- 3.1 Self-Assessment Sheet: students evaluate their learning against the lesson objectives

Ideas for starters

1. Use the starter from the *Student Book*. If students have experienced any of the situations personally, encourage them to take themselves back to those emotions if they are comfortable doing so. If not, alternative scenarios could be suggested.
2. Think, pair, share: what is 'fate'?
3. Play the chorus of "Karma Chameleon" by Culture Club and challenge students to suggest a range of possible answers to what the word 'karma' means. For example, does it mean 'What we do changes depending on where we are', 'Life is ever changing', 'Fate has different challenges for us', or 'Our actions affect our lives'?

Activity guidance

- Before using the starter in the *Student Book*, if students have not experienced 'focused thinking' or 'led meditation' style activities before, explain that they need to clear their minds – and that the most important thing is to relax. You could encourage them to close their eyes before imagining those sentences so as to avoid distraction.
- Ask students to share their responses to Activity **2**, either in pairs or within a group (an opportunity for peer-assessment).

Ideas for plenaries

1. Use the Reflection from the *Student Book*. This could be extended to become a 'Life Plan' activity in which students reflect on what they want their life to look like by creating a diagram or diary entry.
2. Conduct 'The Big Debate'. Ask some of the class to take on the roles of:
    - a Hindu who follows ahimsa
    - an atheist
    - an agnostic
    - a presenter who asks 'Why do innocent creatures and people suffer?'

    Follow-up questions could be 'Can karmic debt explain all the suffering on Earth? How or why not?'. Audience members can also give their views about the same questions – either when asked by the presenter or by raising hands.
3. Suggest that students take on the Ahimsa Challenge: 'How long can you manage without there being any violence in your actions, your words, your speech and your thoughts?'. This means no hitting, no swearing, no saying bad things, and even not wishing anyone ill or thinking badly of them! Ask them what have they learned about themselves from taking this challenge.
4. Ask students to prepare an assembly or news report, or hold a class debate, about the statement: 'Money cannot buy you happiness'.

Further class and homework activities

1. Ask students to 'pass the ball' in groups, with the aim of not being the person holding the ball when the buzzer/bell sounds at the end of a set period of time. They have to take it in turns to name and explain a word from the Useful Words for this unit when they are holding the ball, then pass it to the next person.
2. As a homework task, students should learn the Useful Words and definitions explored in the *Student Book* unit for a quick quiz next lesson.
3. 3.1 Karma Interactive Activity on the *Hinduism OxBox Online*.
4. 3.1 Wealth and Fame Worksheet on the *Hinduism OxBox Online*.
5. Further suggestions on page 58 of this book.

3.2 A Rough Guide to Festivals and Rituals

The unit in brief

This unit looks at how puja may be performed at home and at three popular festivals that many British Hindus celebrate annually.

Key ideas

- Popular Hindu festivals and rituals and key features associated with them
- The purpose of ritual in faiths and the symbolism behind some actions
- People's 'need' for rituals

Useful Words

Janmashtami, puja, Raksha Bandhan

Skills practised

- Design: creating a festival
- Research: investigating more about Hindu festivals
- Literacy: learning new words

Resources

- 3.2 Rituals Film Clip A: Neha and Nirav Dave share what happens at Raksha Bandhan
- 3.2 Rituals Film Clip B: Nirav Dave asks his great aunt about Sitla Saatam customs
- 3.2 Rituals Film Clip C: Nisha and Nirav Patani discuss Janmashtami
- 3.2 Festivals Interactive Activity: students identify features of Hindu festivals and rituals
- 3.2 Film Worksheet: students assess their understanding of the case study film clips by linking ideas to the *Student Book*
- 3 Image Gallery: a useful gallery of photos and film stills from the chapter
- 3.2 Lesson Player: a ready-to-go presentation with built-in resources and teacher notes
- 3.2 Self-Assessment Sheet: students evaluate their learning against the lesson objectives

Ideas for starters

1. Ask students to think back to any religious rituals that they have observed or taken part in at school, home or a place of worship. They should consider why they were there and how it felt, and why the people involved (e.g. a couple getting married in church) wanted a religious ceremony for the event.

2. Play a selection of scenes from films and/or soaps featuring religious ceremonies. Try to include a range of faiths, e.g. the Sikh wedding in Bend it Like Beckham. Ask students to consider why people (sometimes not particularly religious people) wish to have a religious ritual to mark special occasions in their lives.

Activity guidance

- For Activity 2, which asks students to choose and investigate at least one Hindu festival, you could suggest one, e.g. Holi. Ask students to present their research findings in small groups or to the whole class.

Ideas for plenaries

1. Role-play a Hindu ritual with the class. Before starting, you could make it clear to the class that participation neither 'makes' anyone a Hindu, nor offends the ritual if the intention is to educate. A good suggestion might be Raksha Bandhan – the 'blessing bond' for brothers and sisters.

   You will need some kumkum powder made into a paste with water (or some red face paint), a small amount of uncooked rice, some sweets or dried fruit, and enough 'rakhis' or friendship bracelets for half the students in the class.

   Half the students have to choose (or are allocated) a 'brother', and they then perform the ritual:
   - placing a dot on their forehead with the kumkum/face paint and rice (using the third finger of the right hand)
   - feeding them a sweet
   - tying a rakhi/bracelet around their right hand.
2. Compare 'My Festival' ideas from *Student Book* Activity 1 and vote for one that the class would want to celebrate at a later date. An extension could be to actually plan and hold the festival as a class event.

Further class and homework activities

1. Ask students to make a rhyme to help them remember the useful words from this unit of the *Student Book*, to help them in a test next lesson.
2. 3.2 Festivals Interactive Activity on the *Hinduism OxBox Online*.
3. 3.2 Film Worksheet on the *Hinduism OxBox Online*.
4. 3.2 Rituals Film Clips A, B and C on the *Hinduism OxBox Online*.
5. Further suggestions on page 58 of this book.

3.3 Special Feature: A Family Affair

The unit in brief

This case study unit explores the importance of family in Hindu culture, and the ways in which some Hindus share faith with each other.

Key ideas

- The importance of family in Hinduism
- Recognizing that participating in faith events is a way of learning
- Some Hindu beliefs about life and death

Useful Words

bhajan, extended family

Skills practised

- Empathy: linking own experience and feelings about family to case studies
- Personal reflection: considering views about death and remembrance
- Oracy: sharing thoughts verbally and through debate

Resources

- 3.3 Family Film Clip A: Miran and his mother talk about family gatherings and feasts
- 3.3 Family Film Clip B: the Dave family discuss what they learn from and like about family gatherings
- 3.3 Gatherings Interactive Activity: students consider the reasons for Hindu family gatherings
- 3.3 Film Worksheet: students assess their understanding of the case study film clips by linking ideas to the *Student Book*
- 3 Image Gallery: a useful gallery of photos and film stills from the chapter
- 3.3 Lesson Player: a ready-to-go presentation with built-in resources and teacher notes
- 3.3 Self-Assessment Sheet: students evaluate their learning against the lesson objectives

Ideas for starters

1. Use the starter from the *Student Book*.
2. Ask students to list or mind-map who they would say their family is.
3. Ask students, in pairs, to discuss what they think the difference is between 'nuclear' and 'extended' families.
4. Present images of different 'special events', e.g. birthday celebrations, weddings, graduation ceremony, Christmas, Divali, someone in hospital with visitors, funeral, new baby. Ask students to consider who is likely to be at the events and why. 'Family' is likely to be one of the answers.

5. Present images of, or provide a list of famous families and ask students to decide what they have in common. Try to vary how popular the families are to give some challenge, e.g. Simpson, Walton, Adamms, Weasley. This could be a group task.

Activity Guidance

- You could ask students to 'send' the social networking post they composed for Activity **1**, either as notes or by talking in pairs. Other students could be invited to comment on the posts.
- You could follow up Activity **4** by asking students to share and compare their 'pros and cons birds' and discuss some of the responses as a class.

Ideas for plenaries

1. Use the Reflection from the *Student Book*.
2. Ask students to compose a poem or prayer that could be used as a bhajan. They could present their composition as a beautifully decorated written piece, or make a digital/CD recording, or recite/chant/sing it to the class.
3. Ask students to reflect on how much time they spend with their own families. Set them a personal challenge of joining in more with whole family events, or making time for family members they don't often speak to.
4. If you deem it appropriate for your class, you could explore the area of death further. You could explain to students that many non-Hindus, adults included, do not like to talk about death. However, many Hindus believe that sharing thoughts about death with family members can make difficult times easier. They might say that questions such as: 'Do we donate their organs or not?', 'How should we dispose of the body?' and 'What kind of funeral should we have?' could have been avoided if they had already talked about them with their loved one during their lifetime. You could invite students to consider any of these questions for themselves in groups.

Further class and homework activities

1. 3.3 Interactive Activity on the *Hinduism OxBox Online.*
2. 3.3 Family Film Clips A and B on the *Hinduism OxBox Online.*
3. 3.3 Film Worksheet on the *Hinduism OxBox Online.*
4. Further suggestions on page 58 of this book.

3.4 Love, Love, Love! Expressing Faith

The unit in brief

This unit covers different types of love – in general life and as expressions of devotion to the Divine in Hinduism. Students consider whether any one type of love or expression of it is more valuable than others.

Key ideas

- What 'love' means, with reference to the Greek terms agape, eros, philos and storge
- The Hindu concepts of bhakti, karma and gnaan
- The relative merits of different types and expressions of love
- Links between religious beliefs and people's behaviour

Useful Words

agape, bhakti, eros, gnaan, karma, philos, storge

Skills practised

- Empathy: engaging with own and others' experiences of different types and expressions of love
- Self-awareness: reflecting on what really matters and why
- Working with others: engaging constructively in group activities
- Communication: getting across views persuasively

Resources

- 3.4 Love Interactive Activity: students link key terms to their definitions
- 3.4 Expressing Faith Worksheet: students sort ways of expressing faith in a Venn diagram
- 3 Image Gallery: a useful gallery of photos and film stills from the chapter
- 3.4 Lesson Player: a ready-to-go presentation with built-in resources and teacher notes
- 3.4 Self-Assessment Sheet: students evaluate their learning against the lesson objectives

Ideas for starters

1. Use the starter from the *Student Book*. You could choose to play an online version of The Beatles, "All You Need is Love", or alternatively students could choose their own song.
2. Present a range of pictures showing different expressions of love (romantic, charity work, sports events, worship, parent/child hugging, friends). Ask students to consider how the different types of love shown make individuals feel.

Ideas for plenaries

1. As another example of bhakti, play students a version of "My Sweet Lord" by George Harrison. Ask students to listen actively and answer the questions: 'How does the composer feel about God? What kind of words might he use to describe the Divine?'.
2. Use the Reflection from the *Student Book*. As well as being an independent reflection, students could share within pairs.
3. Ask students to imagine that they are part of a group applying for a lottery grant for a project linked to how you show love for the Divine. Divide the class into three groups and ask them to prepare a presentation detailing the benefits to young Hindus, the local community and society at large, of their proposal. Encourage the groups to use a range of media, and to consider the skills of group members when deciding who does what, to help create a successful bid.

The Proposals

- An evening class where people of all ages can learn how to meditate and practice yoga (an ancient Hindu form of exercise, mind control and worship). The bidders believe that the class will not only promote good health and physical well-being, but will also enable young people in particular to find a focus and learn self-discipline.
- A Hindu youth centre where young Hindus (and anyone else) can learn to play Indian instruments and sing popular bhajan (hymns). There will also be lessons in the story-telling tradition of dance, which is an acceptable form of worship.
- A project proposed by the local mandir to clean up and maintain the local park. It is currently full of rubbish, and is a place where some young people hang out smoking. This puts off other people from going there.

As an extension, ask students to imagine that they are in charge of deciding which project receives a Lottery grant. They need to consider the relative merits of each bid and how it may benefit young believers, the local community and society in general.

Ask the groups to present their verdict as a two-minute publicity statement for the press, explaining the merits of the victorious bid and why the other two were not successful.

Further class and homework activities

1. Use 3 Image Gallery to show students pictures of the four Greek words for love. Ask them how many different types of love they can come up with. Would they suggest any other categories?
2. 3.4 Interactive Activity on the *Hinduism OxBox Online.*
3. 3.4 Expressing Faith Worksheet on the *Hinduism OxBox Online.*
4. Further suggestions on page 58 of this book.

3.5 What's My Role? Hindu Life Stages

The unit in brief

This unit explains the concept of varnashrama dharma, and also explores how it affects real people through case studies. There is a particular focus on the four Hindu stages of life (ashrama) and on dharma (duty).

Key ideas

- What some Hindus mean by dharma, and how this concept can affect their lives
- The four ashrama and how they apply to Hindus' lives.
- The value of having set goals and duties in life
- Reflecting on students' own place and purpose in the world

Skills practised

- Personal reflection: thinking about how the issues studied relate to own life
- Working with others: building and sharing understanding through mature pair work
- Communication: expressing thoughts verbally and learning using role-play, interview techniques and discussion
- Decision making: coming to an informed conclusion using evidence and thinking skills

Resources

- 3.5 Ashrama Film Clip A: Nisha Patani considers the four ashrama
- 3.5 Ashrama Film Clip B: Miran and Mrs Morris discuss their views on Hindu life stages
- 3.5 Stages Interactive Activity: students must correctly order ashrama based on a description
- 3.5 Film Worksheet: students assess their understanding of the case study film clips by linking ideas to the *Student Book*
- 3 Image Gallery: a useful gallery of photos and film stills from the chapter
- 3.5 Lesson Player: a ready-to-go presentation with built-in resources and teacher notes
- 3.5 Self-Assessment Sheet: students evaluate their learning against the lesson objectives

Ideas for starters

1. Use the starter from the Student Book.
2. Ask students to list or mind-map reasons why they think you are a teacher; and/or why adults at home are in certain careers/ professions; and/or why adults at home do other jobs (e.g. keeping the house clean and tidy, preparing meals, helping out at scouts or as a sports coach).

Ideas for plenaries

1. Use the Reflection from the *Student Book*.
2. Ask students the question: 'Is doing what you want better or worse for society than doing what you should?'. Ask them to come up with scenarios that might support each outcome.
3. **a)** Following on from the 'life map' starter, ask students to create a life map highlighting the Hindu ashramas, including some examples of how the first two in particular could be completed.
   b) Ask them to create their own version of the ashramas (there can be more than four if they like).
   c) What should people do at different stages of life and why? Students could present their ideas as a PowerPoint presentation, a poster/diagram, or a magazine article.
   d) An alternative to this would be to ask students to compose an article about why they might argue that 'Anyone should be able to do anything at any time of life'.
4. **a)** Ask students to investigate the fourth stage of sannyasin and create a fact-file or spider diagram detailing what this stage involves.
   b) They could extend this by suggesting reasons why many Hindus do not get to (or even attempt to) complete the fourth stage.
5. **a)** Ask students to conduct a survey (within the class or wider school community) to see what young people at the school think being a student means (the responsibilities involved and what's good/bad about it), and how many plan/expect to marry and/or have children, with their reasons why. (You might need to provide a framework for the questionnaires where required, but encourage students to design their own questions and format to best fit the brief.)
   b) Students could present their findings as a series of graphs.
   c) They could also analyse the results and share what they reveal about the attitudes of young people at the school and some reasons behind them.

Further class and homework activities

1. Use 3 Image Gallery on the *Hinduism OxBox Online* to show the four pictures representing the ashrama to students. Ask them what they think they might represent and why. Do they think their own lives will have distinct stages like this?
2. Students should learn the four ashramas explored in this *Student Book* unit for a quick quiz next lesson.
3. 3.5 Stages Interactive Activity on the *Hinduism OxBox Online*.
4. 3.5 Ashrama Film Clips A and B on the *Hinduism OxBox Online*.
5. 3.5 Film Worksheet on the *Hinduism OxBox Online*.
6. Further suggestions on page 58 of this book.

3.6 Wonderful Ways to Worship: Yoga, Dance and Songs

The unit in brief

This unit examines some different ways in which Hindus (and others) worship, with reference to case study families. There are opportunities for experiential learning, through participation in meditation and yoga.

Key ideas

- Hindus worship in a variety of ways
- What it means to connect with the Divine in worship
- How talents can be used to make the world a better place

Skills practised

- Personal reflection: taking part in meditation and yoga
- Thinking: interpreting and applying scripture to practice and considering what's really important about worship
- Empathy: connecting to experiences shared by case studies

Resources

- 3.6 Worship Film Clip A: the Morris family worshipping at their shrine
- 3.6 Worship Film Clip B: Gaiatri doing yoga
- 3.6 Worship Film Clip C: a tour of a mandir
- 3.6 Meditation Audio Clip: a led meditation for you to use with students
- 3.6 Acts and Living Interactive Activity: students decide which ways of worship are lifestyle choices
- 3.6 Film Worksheet: students assess their understanding of the case study film clips by linking ideas to the *Student Book*
- 3 Image Gallery: a useful gallery of photos and film stills from the chapter
- 3.6 Lesson Player: a ready-to-go presentation with built-in resources and teacher notes
- 3.6 Self-Assessment Sheet: students evaluate their learning against the lesson objectives

Ideas for starters

1. Use the starter from the *Student Book*. You could ask students to create a spider diagram as an individual response, work in groups on big bits of paper, or hold a class discussion and make notes on the board.

2. Show the class some clips or pictures of different ways to worship, e.g. voluntary or charity work, dance, artwork, sportsperson showing faith pre-/post-event. Ask students what connects these images. Alternatively, ask students to sort each picture or clip as 'worship' and 'not worship' and discuss their reasoning in small groups.

Ideas for plenaries

1. Ask students to create a mind-map of the many ways Hindu may worship. Then ask them to compare with a partner and explore reasons for any similarities and differences.
2. Ask students to research the use of dance to worship in Hinduism. A good example would be the Hindu festival of Navaratri.
   - **a)** You could show students videos such as 'Celebrating Navaratri' on the BBC's Learning Zone website. You could then ask them: 'Do you think the element of fun involved in Navaratri celebrations makes faith more attractive for many Hindus?'
   - **b)** This could be extended by asking students to make a 'Fun Festivals' chart. For example, paint fights at Holi, or rocking baby Krishna in his cradle and staying up late at Janmashtami.
3. Ask students to compose a piece of music or poetry, or create a dance or work of art showing either their own sense of the Divine, or a Hindu understanding of the Divine (using Chapter 1 of the *Student Book*).
4. Ask students to think about the fact that some schools are required to have a 'collective act of worship, broadly Christian in nature'. Using their learning from this unit, ask them whether they think this is a way to set a good example to young people and help their spiritual growth, or whether it puts some young people off religion and/or exploring their own spirituality? Ask them to consider examples that agree with both sides of the argument and use them effectively in a debate about the issue.

Further class and homework activities

1. Use 3.6 Meditation Audio Clip to lead a meditation in the class.
   - **a)** Ask students to reflect upon their experience of meditation by writing a social networking post.
   - **b)** Ask them to deepen their reflection as a diary entry, poem, or piece of art.
   - **c)** If it's something they already do, ask students to share *why* they meditate. If it was new to them, ask them to explore how it affected their thoughts and feelings.
2. 3.6 Acts and Living Interactive Activity on the *Hinduism OxBox Online.*
3. 3.6 Worship Film Clips A, B and C on the *Hinduism OxBox Online.*
4. 3.6 Film Worksheet on the *Hinduism OxBox Online.*
5. Further suggestions on page 58 of this book.

Chapter 3 Further Suggestions

These suggestions are addressed directly to students.

3.1 Karma: A Sense of Purpose!

1 The concept of karmic debt explains suffering for some Hindus, but what other reasons can you think of for why people suffer? List or mind-map your thoughts. */**/***

2 **a** Investigate the work and beliefs of someone who really 'lives with purpose'. It might be someone you know personally (e.g. a relative or neighbour), or someone famous (e.g. a Paralympian or Olympian, explorer, inventor or news reporter).

b Create a profile about what motivates and inspires them. Try to find out if, and how, religious belief plays a part in their approach to life.

c Explore and evaluate how they have dealt with 'bad karma' in their lives and where they create 'good karma'. ***

3 Design (and make, if possible) a 'Karmic Consequences' game that illustrates how karmic debt works. You could base it on an existing game that you alter a bit (e.g. Snakes and Ladders or Monopoly), or get really creative and invent a game of your own. */**/***

3.2 A Rough Guide to Festivals and Rituals

1 Investigate how at least one Hindu festival is celebrated (either just in Britain or in Britain *and* in parts of India) and create your own 'Rough Guide to [name of festival chosen]'. There are lots to choose from, so try to do a different one from your friends! Some other examples are Holi, Navaratri and Ramnavami, but you could use an example from the *Student Book* and add to it. */**/***

2 Homework: Design or make some rakhis to use as examples in class, give to a friend or family member, or wear yourself. */**/***

3 Compare and contrast ways in which Lord Krishna's birthday is celebrated at Janmashtami with how Jesus' birthday is celebrated at Christmas. */**

3.3 Special Feature: A Family Affair

1 If there is a Mother's Day and Father's Day, should other family members have a 'day' too? If 'yes', who and when? If 'no', why not? Share your thoughts as a comment for a social networking site (no more than 140 characters). */**/***

2 In Mexico there is a 'Day of the Dead', when people commemorate loved ones who have died with shrines dedicated to them, including candles, flowers and the person's favourite foods. This is a happy time rather than a time of mourning and grief.

a Compare these Mexican traditions with how the Dave family commemorated their loved ones who had died at the bhajan, and reflect on reasons for any similarities and differences. **/***

b Explore further how the Day of the Dead is commemorated. Make a 'Guide to the Day of the Dead' using ICT, written, or verbal presentation skills. */**/***

3.4 Love, Love, Love! Expressing Faith

1 Design a range of Love Hearts sweets with messages to show that love is more than just eros (romance). */**/***

2 Homework: Track how often you say 'I love...' in a day and reflect on how much is real love (of any type) and how many times you were just using the phrase without really thinking. Do you notice any patterns? */**/***

3.5 What's My Role? Hindu Life Stages

1 Most Hindus do not complete the fourth ashrama, which is to become a sannyasin and leave behind the material world (including everything they own and their family and friends), so that their total focus is on the Divine and on achieving moksha. Investigate how some sannyasin live, what they do and why. */**/***

2 Homework:

a Speak to family and friends about the influence and role of grandparents in their lives. How many people include: guidance, teaching right from wrong, and giving advice? */**/***

b Does your research suggest that most grand-parents fulfill the third ashrama anyway, or is it something that Hindu grandparents would have to really think about and work at doing well? **/***

3.6 Wonderful Ways to Worship: Yoga, Dance and Songs

1 Choose a story from Hindu scripture and design a way to deliver it to people who cannot read. You could create a dance, plan a series of carvings to decorate a mandir, compose a song, or anything creative that gets the story across. */**/***

2 Should worship be part of public events, or is it completely personal? The legal requirement for schools to have 'a daily act of worship' is a cause of debate. Research this issue further and prepare a speech or article that explains different views and justifies your own conclusion.***

Chapter 3 Assessment

Assessment in the *Student Book*

You will find an assessment task at the end of every chapter which focuses on AT2. In this chapter, the task asks students to create a detailed mind-map which explains some ways in which Hindus may express their spirituality, and establishes connections between different practices.

In the *Student Book* (and on the supporting worksheets), you'll find guidance about levels of assessment that you can use to help your students understand what their work should include. You could ask them to use these criteria for self- or peer- assessment once they've completed the task.

Living Faiths Assessment

Student Book
- Assessment Task
- Levels Guidance

OxBox Online
- Auto-Marked Test
- Assessment Task Presentation
- Assessment Worksheets

Assessment Task for Chapter 3 (pages **46–47** of the *Hinduism Student Book*)

Objectives
- Explore and explain some ways in which Hindus may express their spirituality
- Develop thinking skills by establishing connections between different practices
- Develop creativity and presentational skills

Task
Your aim is to create a detailed mind-map of ways in which different expressions of the Hindu faith are connected, using the Dave family bhajan as your starting point. Use the questions below to help you plan your mind-map.
- Why did the Dave family gather on that occasion?
- How do the other Hindu families express their faith?
- In what ways might the younger members of the family: (a) participate in; and (b) learn about some aspects of Hinduism?

Assessment in *OxBox Online*

On the *Hinduism OxBox Online*, you'll find resources to use when introducing the assessment task to the class.

You can use the *Chapter 3 Assessment Task Presentation* as a front-of-class tool to help your students unpack the assessment criteria, and understand what is expected of them.

Chapter 3 Assessment Worksheets accompany the task, so that once you finish the presentation, your students can easily get started.

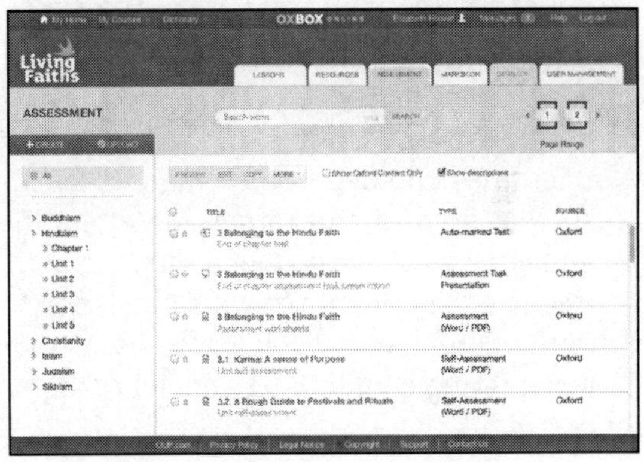

▲ Assessment resources for Chapter 3 on the *Hinduism Oxbox Online*

Auto-marked tests

The *Hinduism OxBox Online* also contains auto-marked tests for each chapter to help save you time setting questions and marking for AT1. The test for this chapter contains 15 questions and will take most students about half an hour. Test results are automatically stored in the markbook.

Digital markbook

A markbook and a reporting function complete the *OxBox Online* assessment package, so you can keep all your students' test results and assessment scores in one place. This can include the auto-marked tests as well as pieces of work you or the students have marked by hand.

Chapter 4 Overview
Raising Questions, Exploring Answers

Helping you deliver Key Stage 3 RE

This chapter addresses the following areas of the Programme of Study:

Key concepts

Values and commitments

- Understand how moral values and a sense of obligation can come from beliefs and experience
- Evaluate their own and others' values in order to make informed, rational and imaginative choices

Key processes

Learning about religion

- Evaluate how religious beliefs and teachings inform answers to ultimate questions and ethical issues
- Analyse religious beliefs, arguments and ideas

Learning from religion

- Express their own beliefs and ideas, using a variety of forms of creative expression and reasoned arguments

The big picture

These are the key ideas behind this chapter:

- Dilemmas and decisions. Religious teachings, such as ahimsa and karma, can affect the beliefs and choices of some young Hindus about moral issues. Many Hindus find it a challenge to balance faith, culture and social pressures, as well as interpreting conflicting or unclear religious teachings.
- Focus on food and Ayurveda. Hindu teachings reveal that the effects of certain types of food can affect character and nature (and vice versa). Food features in many festivals, and the practice of fasting is also important in Hinduism.
- Many Hindus have strong views about environmental and animal issues. For instance, believing that animals have souls affects the views of many Hindus. The vegetarian debate is also prominent.

Chapter outline

Use this to give students a mental road map of the chapter:

4.1 The Four Aims in Life – explores artha, dharma, kama and moksha as highlighted in some Hindu scripture and examines how to define honest wealth

4.2 How do I Decide What's Right? Difficult Decisions! – introduces the idea of ethical or moral problems and decisions, including case studies

4.3 How do I Decide What's Right? Some Dilemmas of Modern Life – examines particular moral dilemmas that young Hindus might face in modern Britain

4.4 Are You What You Eat? – discusses links between diet and personality and uses case studies to explain fasting and certain Hindu dietary choices

4.5 Special Feature: Food Glorious Food! – introduces Ayurveda and makes links between food and health using case studies

4.6 Animal Magic – links Hindu beliefs to issues of animal treatment

4.7 Planet or People? Caring for the Environment – Uses case studies to consider Hindu beliefs about the environment

Opportunities for assessment

Summative assessments on the *Hinduism OxBox Online* include auto-marked tests, interactive activities, and self-assessment worksheets.

The end-of-chapter assessment task in the *Student Book* provides formative assessment. Supporting materials for the assessment task can be found on the *Hinduism OxBox Online*, such as the Assessment Task Presentation and the related worksheets.

There are other opportunities for assessment too. For example, you could use some of the activities or reflection points throughout each *Student Book* unit, or some of the 'Further Suggestions' at the end of this chapter.

Getting ready for this chapter

- Obtain current media examples of the moral issues raised by this chapter, such as the laws on euthanasia. These moral issues are constantly featured in the press in some way.
- For the food features, if you can bring in some real food items, such as mint, cloves and ginger, and allow students (being careful about allergy issues) to at least touch and smell the items, if not taste them, it will really open their minds and senses!

Objectives and outcomes for this chapter

Objectives	Unit	Outcomes
Most students will:		Most students will be able to:
• develop understanding of the aims in life held by many Hindus • explore the dilemmas caused by artha • consider the meaning of life.	**4.1**	• identify examples of artha, dharma, kama and moksha • debate what 'earning wealth honestly' involves • discuss the meaning of life.
• develop understanding about what ethical decisions are • explain how Hindus draw on their religion to find answers to ethical problems • explore what influences them in making ethical decisions.	**4.2**	• explain, with examples, what ethical or moral issues are • explain the role of Hinduism in addressing moral problems • share and justify own views about the issues of euthanasia and just war.
• consider some of the difficulties involved in being a young Hindu in the UK today • reflect upon their own morality – what really matters and why • identify some links between Hindu teachings and morality.	**4.3**	• identify some dilemmas where Hindu culture/faith and personal/social views may be at odds • explain their own moral values and the reasons for them • discriminate between solely religious 'rules' and those which are religious *and* moral.
• analyse some Hindu beliefs about diet and personality • examine and explain why many Hindus are vegetarian • examine what they eat and how it impacts their life.	**4.4**	• explain and evaluate the concepts of satva, rajas and tamas • understand reasons for not eating meat • identify the saatvic, rajasic and tamasic aspects of their diets.
• make links between food and health • develop understanding about the Vedic tradition of Ayurveda • investigate the relevance of ancient wisdom in the modern world.	**4.5**	• identify some foods and their health benefits • understand the philosophy that our mind, body and spirit are affected by what we consume • identify similarities and differences between 'modern' and Ayurvedic health advice.
• investigate how animals are treated by humans • apply Hindu teachings to how animals are treated • make informed decisions about issues to do with animals.	**4.6**	• identify some ways in which humans mistreat animals • evaluate whether Hindu teachings allow using animals for entertainment or medicine • justify their own views using reasoning and examples.
• examine some Hindu beliefs about the environment • evaluate their own impact on the Earth • analyse the pros and cons of technological advancement.	**4.7**	• identify some Hindu teachings about the Earth • Identify ways to reduce their carbon footprint • give examples to support both sides of the technology argument.

4.1 The Four Aims in Life

The unit in brief

This unit explores the meaning of life, including the concepts of artha (honest wealth) and kama (sensual pleasure). It also builds on previous learning about moksha (liberation from the cycle of rebirth) and dharma (duty).

Key ideas

- The four main aims in life held by many Hindus
- Some of the dilemmas caused by artha
- Some consideration by students of the meaning of life

Useful Words

artha, dharma, kama, moksha

Skills practised

- Debating: defending a particular viewpoint about what honestly earned wealth means using reasoning and examples
- Thinking: analysing and evaluating the problems that may be associated with wealth from several angles
- Communication: getting across understanding of issues effectively and expressing their own views persuasively
- Presentation: using a variety of media to explore arguments about the meaning of life
- Reflection: considering what the aim of life is and why

Resources

- 4.1 Aims Interactive Activity: students match life aims with their definitions
- 4.1 Quotations Worksheet: students assess their level of agreement with quotations about the purpose of life
- 4 Image Gallery: a useful gallery of photos and film stills from the chapter
- 4.1 Lesson Player: a ready-to-go presentation with built-in resources and teacher notes
- 4.1 Self-Assessment Sheet: students evaluate their learning against the lesson objectives

Ideas for starters

1. Use the starter in the *Student Book*. As a lighter way into the topic, you could show an online clip from *The Hitchhicker's Guide to the Galaxy* – or read from Chapter 27 of the book – the scene where '42' is discovered to be the answer to the meaning of life.
2. Ask students to share their ambitions in pairs, groups and as a class. Then ask them to discuss whether 'ambition' is the same as 'purpose'.

3. Play a section from a love song, or read a stanza from a poem, that features the sentiment 'without you, life has no meaning' in some form. Ask students to reflect on what the singer or poet means by those words.

Activity guidance

Some students may link kama with the book *Kama Sutra* (which can be translated as 'Rules about Sensual Pleasure'), if they have heard of it. If so, you could use the opportunity to clear up confusion and point out to students that the *Kama Sutra* includes guidance about respect, tenderness and care for the partner – so there is emotional and spiritual pleasure given and gained, not just physical. The *Kama Sutra* is part of a larger set of texts entitled 'Kama Shashtra' – guidance on stimulating and fulfilling all of the senses. Therefore, art, food and music are as much a part of seeking kama as lovemaking is.

Ideas for plenaries

1. Use the Reflection as the basis of a class debate.
2. Give students the following statement: 'Dharma, artha and kama are a Hindu's aims for everyday life, but moksha is release from the cycle of life itself; so moksha must be the *real* meaning of life for Hindus!'. Ask students to move to a designated part of the room, depending on whether they:
   - A – agree
   - D – disagree
   - N – are not sure

   'A's and 'D's can also have the challenge of persuading those 'in the middle' to join them by using intelligent reasoning.
3. For an extension activity, you could ask students to investigate the thoughts of a famous philosopher or theologian about the meaning of life. They could share their findings as either a speech on the topic or a creative response. An extra challenge would be to summarize their views as a social networking post written by each thinker. An interesting next step would be for students to examine each other's work and decide who they would follow on a social networking site, based on what they have said about life.

Further class and homework activities

1. Students should learn the four Hindu aims in life explored in this *Student Book* unit, along with definitions, for a quick quiz next lesson.
2. As another homework, you could ask students to research some quotations about the meaning of life which they identify with and to create a 'Top Four on What I Live For!'. A useful starter to the next lesson would be for students to share and explain their choices in pairs or small groups.
3. 4.1 Aims Interactive Activity on the *Hinduism OxBox Online*.
4. 4.1 Quotations Worksheet on the *Hinduism OxBox Online*.
5. Further suggestions on page 76 of this book.

4.2 How do I Decide What's Right? Difficult Decisions!

The unit in brief

This unit analyses how some Hindus make ethical decisions, and also how individuals may decide what's right and wrong.

Key ideas

- What ethical decisions are and what they involve
- Different Hindus have a range of responses to most ethical questions
- The development of students' own views about important ethical issues

Useful Words

ethics/ethical, euthanasia

Skills practised

- Thinking: exploring a range of 'difficult' issues and being able to justify views
- Reasoning and decision making: coming to informed conclusions
- Working with others: demonstrate understanding, listening and thinking skills through role-play and debate
- Interpretation and evaluation: understanding a range of scripture and teachings

Resources

- 4.2 Right or Wrong Interactive Activity: students consider how often actions are right or wrong
- 4.2 Punishments Worksheet: Students assess what level of punishment certain acts should deserve
- 4.2 Scripture Audio Clip: readings of the scriptural quotations in this unit
- 4 Image Gallery: a useful gallery of photos and film stills from the chapter
- 4.2 Lesson Player: a ready-to-go presentation with built-in resources and teacher notes
- 4.2 Self-Assessment Sheet: students evaluate their learning against the lesson objectives

Ideas for starters

1. Use the starter from the *Student Book*. You could extend this by using a different ethical statement. For example: 'It is never acceptable to declare war on another nation' or 'Abortion should be made illegal in Britain'. The class could demonstrate their views by sitting/standing according to how strongly they agree or disagree.
2. List the Useful Words from the *Student Book* on the board without definitions and ask students to discuss what they think they mean in pairs or groups.

3. Ask: 'What do we mean by the terms "right" and "wrong"? Can anything be totally right or wrong across time, geography and society, or does it always depend on the context?' Students could think, pair and share.

Activity guidance

- Once students have prepared arguments surrounding an ethical issue, you could stage a TV-style debate. Hold the show with individuals taking on the roles of faith representatives and campaigners.
- You might wish to compare Hindu teachings about key issues with those from other religions. See Unit 5.4 in the *Islam Student Book*.

Ideas for plenaries

1. Ask students to compose their own definitions of the Useful Words in the *Student Book* for a 'Teen Dictionary', including an example or scenario to illustrate each term.
2. Ask students to list or make a spider diagram of places and people where a Hindu could get advice about the ethical issues of just war and euthanasia. Ask: 'How does a Hindu decide what to do if the sources give different advice?' For example, Gandhi says 'no war' but the Bhagavad Gita says sometimes it is necessary to use violence to protect people.
3. As an extension to the starter in the *Student Book*, you could ask students whether moral or ethical truth is always 'relative' to the situation, or is there moral or ethical truth 'out there'? If the latter, where? How do we know what it is? Does the fact that most people agree about some things (such as torture for entertainment being wrong) 'prove' that there is a God (of some description)? How?
4. As an extension task, you could ask students to analyse the two quotes from the Bhagavad Gita in detail. What do they understand by 'righteous war' and do they think war is ever justifiable? See Unit 4.6 in the *Christianity Student Book* for a definition of 'just war'. You may wish to play students 4.2 Scripture Audio Clip to aid their thinking.

Further class and homework activities

1. Use 4.2 Right or Wrong Interactive Activity as a starting point for this unit. There is a range of situations to be discussed. Share and discuss reasons for responses.
2. You could ask students, as a homework task, to discuss with family and friends where ethical beliefs come from. Are people's life experiences very similar or quite different? Does having a religious background help and why or why not?
3. 4.2 Punishments Worksheet on the *Hinduism OxBox Online*.
4. Further suggestions on page 76 of this book.

4.3 How do I Decide What's Right? Some Dilemmas of Modern Life

The unit in brief

This unit will explore what moral decisions and dilemmas are, and specifically how modern life may cause additional dilemmas for young Hindus.

Key ideas

- Some of the moral difficulties faced by young Hindus in the UK today
- Links between Hindu teachings and morality
- Students' own morality – what really matters and why

Useful Words

morality, moral dilemma

Skills practised

- Thinking: considering a moral dilemma and using reasoning to come up with a response
- Self-awareness: reflecting upon own values and influences when faced with a difficult decision

Resources

- 4.3 Dilemmas Interactive Activity A: students assess which 'rules' are moral or religious
- 4.3 Dilemmas Interactive Activity B: students try to solve a difficult dilemma
- 4.3 Ranking Worksheet: students consider the questions one asks when solving a dilemma
- 4 Image Gallery: a useful gallery of photos and film stills from the chapter
- 4.3 Lesson Player: a ready-to-go presentation with built-in resources and teacher notes
- 4.3 Self-Assessment Sheet: students evaluate their learning against the lesson objectives

Ideas for starters

1. Use the starter from the *Student Book*. You could use a different dilemma, or a range of moral dilemmas, as a stimulus for the activity.
2. Ask students to think about and share their own experiences as a follow up to the starter in the *Student Book*.
3. Play a scene from any suitable film or TV programme where someone faces a moral dilemma. Follow this up by asking students to reflect on what factors and considerations might affect their final decision.

Activity guidance

- You could compare Hindu teachings about key moral issues with those from other religions. See Unit 5.4 in the *Islam Student Book* or Unit 4.2 in the *Christianity Student Book*.

Ideas for plenaries

1. Ask students to consider the role of Hindu scripture in helping Hindus to make moral decisions. Many of the stories teach important moral lessons, e.g. the ideals of love and loyalty in the story of Divali. Ask students: 'If Hindus learn moral values through scripture, what happens when there is conflicting information? How do they know what is right?' You could extend this by referring to scripture in other faiths.
2. Present students with the following rules that many Hindus try to follow:
   - Treat all living things with respect. (Many Hindus believe that all living things have a soul.)
   - Honour your elders.
   - Show compassion to those less fortunate than yourself.

   Ask students to think of situations when following these rules might be difficult. For example: 'Does "all living things" include violent humans or animals?', 'What if our elders get it wrong?', 'Does honour mean the same as always obey?', 'Is care for the needy less worthy if the motive is duty rather than real compassion?'.
3. Show students the McDonald's 'Favourites' advert on YouTube. This advert seems to promote eating on the run and while working, but Hindu teachings suggest that how and when Hindus eat being almost as important as what they eat. Use the link to discuss the personal conflict that some Hindus could face between 'doing what everyone else does' and wholly following some faith rules.

Further class and homework activities

1. 4.3 Dilemmas Interactive Activities A and B on the *Hinduism OxBox Online*.

   When discussing the lifeboat moral dilemma scenario in 4.3 Dilemmas Interactive Activity B, you might need to prompt students with key Hindu teachings. For example: 'All life is sacred', 'It is bad karma to take a life', 'It is good karma to end suffering', 'The atman does not die, only the body dies'. This activity should be approached with sensitivity.

   As a homework activity, students could create and carry out a survey of other people's responses to the dilemma. They could then demonstrate their numeracy skills by creating graphs of the results, followed by an analysis of their research.
2. 4.3 Ranking Worksheet on the *Hinduism OxBox Online*.
3. Further suggestions on page 76 of this book.

4.4 Are You What You Eat?

The unit in brief

This unit introduces and explains some food types and food rules from Hindu scripture and culture.

Key ideas

- Teachings about diet and personality from Hindu scripture – how the two are believed to be connected
- Some reasons why many Hindus are vegetarian

Useful Words

fast/fasting, rajas/rajasic, sattva/sattvic, sustainable, tamas/tamasic

Skills practised

- Self-awareness and self-evaluation: being aware of what, why and how we eat
- Working with others: paired and group discussions and analysis
- Empathy and understanding: appreciation of a range of Hindu views and case study beliefs/experiences

Resources

- 4.4 Food Film Clip A: Miran and his mother speak about food
- 4.4 Food Film Clip B: Mrs Morris speaks about being vegetarian
- 4.4 Guna and Varna Interactive Activity: students match terms from the unit to their definitions
- 4.4 Film Worksheet: students assess their understanding of the case study film clips by linking ideas to the *Student Book*
- 4 Image Gallery: a useful gallery of photos and film stills from the chapter
- 4.4 Lesson Player: a ready-to-go presentation with built-in resources and teacher notes
- 4.4 Self-Assessment Sheet: students evaluate their learning against the lesson objectives

Ideas for starters

1. Use the starter from the *Student Book*.
2. If possible, bring in some different types of food and ask students to rate them as red, amber or green, depending on how healthy they are.
3. Show students the percentage figures for what human beings are made up of, e.g. 65% oxygen, 18% carbon, 10% hydrogen, etc. Ask: 'Is this what you are? Is this all you are?'.
4. Get students thinking about how their emotions and sense of well-being might be affected by what they eat and drink. Ask them how they feel when they eat porridge, chips, chocolate, fruit, or their favourite sandwich.

Activity guidance:

- When completing Activity **2**, you could clarify that whilst fasting may have health benefits there are people who should avoid it, e.g. young children and pregnant women.
- You could compare Hindu thinking about food with other religions being studied. See Unit 3.2 in the *Judaism Student Book*, or Unit 3.5 in the *Islam Student Book*.

Ideas for plenaries

1. Ask students to consider the families in the case studies and what the biggest influence is on what they choose to eat or not eat. Then ask them to consider the same question in relation to themselves. They could share their thoughts as a mind-map or a set of concentric circles, with the biggest influence in the centre and lesser influences in the outer rings.
2. For a group challenge, have a picture of a cow in the middle of a big piece of paper (one sheet per group). Give the groups one minute to surround the cow with reasons why Hindus view cows as special. They should use their thinking skills as well as previous learning. Their answers could include: cows are useful for labour (e.g. pulling ploughs or grinding millstones), cow dung is used as fuel, dairy products come from milk, Lord Krishna was a cowherd and is often pictured with cows.
3. If possible, bring in some empty food packaging. Ask students to:
   a) label the packaging with either S, R or T (sattvic, rajasic or tamasic) to show their understanding of food types in Hindu philosophy
   b) look at the ingredients and list any they do not recognize. Do they think that the presence of unknown ingredients makes food more S, R or T? Ask them to share their reasoning in small groups
   c) research what the unknown ingredients are. Would their research affect what they eat in the future? Ask them to reflect upon the reasons for this.

Further class and homework activities

1. As homework, ask students to keep a food diary for one week. They could label what they eat with S, T or R and reflect on whether their moods/behaviour/sense of well-being changes, depending on what they eat.
2. 4.4 Guna and Varna Interactive Activity on the *Hinduism OxBox Online*.
3. 4.4 Food Film Clips A and B on the *Hinduism OxBox Online*.
4. 4.4 Film Worksheet on the *Hinduism OxBox Online*.
5. Further suggestions on page 76 of this book.

4.5 Special Feature: Food Glorious Food!

The unit in brief

This unit introduces and explains Ayurveda (What is it? Why do it?) and ways in which it can relate to and be used by young people today.

Key ideas

- Some connections between food and health
- The Vedic tradition of Ayurveda
- The relevance of ancient wisdom in the modern world

Useful Words

Ayurveda, Ayurvedic, Vedic

Skills practised

- Applying learning to life: recognizing some everyday uses of Ayurveda
- Literacy: being able to use new words correctly and confidently
- Evaluation and reasoning: exploring potential benefits and problems of using Ayurveda in the modern world

Resources

- 4.5 Ayurveda Film Clip: Neha and Nirav's great aunt shares some Ayurveda tips on 'food as medicine'
- 4.5 Properties Interactive Activity: students match the foods to their Ayurvedic properties
- 4.5 Film Worksheet: students assess their understanding of the case study film clips by linking ideas to the *Student Book*
- 4 Image Gallery: a useful gallery of photos and film stills from the chapter
- 4.5 Lesson Player: a ready-to-go presentation with built-in resources and teacher notes
- 4.5 Self-Assessment Sheet: students evaluate their learning against the lesson objectives

Ideas for starters

1. Use the starter from the *Student Book*.
2. If possible, bring in some Ayurvedic foods for a food identification test, e.g. mint, aniseed, cloves, liquorice, aloe vera.
3. Ask the class to discuss, in pairs or small groups, what they could do (apart from taking drugs-based medicines) to help them feel better when they:
   a) have a cold?
   b) have a headache?
   c) have nausea?

Share responses from around the class. Add some of your own if there is not much feedback. For example: (a) keep warm and have honey and lemon; (b) drink some water or have a sleep; and (c) have something with ginger in it or press on pressure points.

Activity guidance

When exploring some of the food wisdom in Hinduism, you could compare it to food rules in other faiths. See Unit 3.2 in the *Judaism Student Book*, or Unit 3.5 in the *Islam Student Book*.

Ideas for plenaries

1. Use the Reflection from the *Student Book*.
2. Ask students why they think food and religion are so closely tied. They could think, pair, share, and then complete an extended writing task.
3. Ask students to think of a problem that could be helped through Ayurveda. They should write a quick note to Auntie Ayurveda describing the problem. Then ask them to swap notes with a partner and compose a response to their partner's note as if they were 'Auntie Ayurveda'.
4. Challenge: Name that Food! Ask students to demonstrate their learning of this topic by using descriptions and actions, but no actual names, to describe as many Ayurvedic foods as they can to a partner in two minutes. The partner has to try to guess what the food is.

Further class and homework activities

1. Students should learn at least three Ayurvedic foods named in this unit, along with what Hindus believe to be their benefits.
2. Ask students to design a radio or TV advert, or poster, with the message, 'Doing your best to keep healthy is a religious, social, *and* moral duty'. Ask them to discuss, in pairs, whether they agree with this statement.
3. Ask students to consider that a large amount of the 'medicines' given to us are actually plant based – they come from naturally-occurring ingredients, e.g. aspirin is made from willow bark. Is the fact that nature provides ways to heal us proof of a caring divine creator who planned the evolution of plants and humans to work together in this way – or is it just coincidence and only proof of human ingenuity?
4. 4.5 Properties Interactive Activity on the *Hinduism OxBox Online*.
5. 4.5 Ayurveda Film Clip on the *Hinduism OxBox Online*.
6. 4.5 Film Worksheet on the *Hinduism OxBox Online*
7. Further suggestions on page 76 of this book

4.6 Animal Magic

The unit in brief

This unit investigates how Hindus view animals. In particular, the issues of cows being held sacred and the use of animals for food, entertainment and experimentation are explored and evaluated.

Key ideas

- The difference between humans and animals (if any)
- How religious beliefs affect the way many humans treat animals
- The issue of eating meat (or not)
- The acceptability (or not) of using animals for human gain

Useful Word

avatar

Skills practised

- Research: finding facts and examples to build understanding of an issue
- Working with others: utilizing skills within a group effectively and efficiently
- Communication: presenting ideas using a range of methods
- Evaluation: coming to an informed decision

Resources

- 4.6 Animals Interactive Activity: students link Hindu behaviours to beliefs about animals
- 4.6 Ganesha Worksheet: students analyse how Ganesha represents the union of humans and animals
- 4 Image Gallery: a useful gallery of photos and film stills from the chapter
- 4.6 Lesson Player: a ready-to-go presentation with built-in resources and teacher notes
- 4.6 Self-Assessment Sheet: students evaluate their learning against the lesson objectives

Ideas for starters

1. Use the starter in the *Student Book* to get students thinking about how they view animals.
2. Display images of animals in different situations (being used for labour, in sport, as a guide dog, in a laboratory, in a zoo, being treated badly, as a happy pet). Students should note the first three words that come to mind for each picture, then share and discuss what the words reveal about how animals are regarded.
3. Talk about your own pet (if you have or have had one) – explain why you have that animal and what it means to you. Ask students to do the same or to share why they do not or would not have pets.

4. Distribute leaflets from a range of pressure groups 'for' and 'against' the issues explored in the activities, and ask students to compare their first impressions.

Activity guidance

- If access to the Internet or books is not readily available for Activity **1**, students could use their learning about Hinduism so far to inform what they think a Hindu might decide about the issue. For instance, many Hindus believe that animals have an atman, and are therefore divine, so they should be treated with the highest respect.
- You could compare their learning on this topic to what is believed by other faiths. See Unit 5.2 in the *Buddhism Student Book*.

Ideas for plenaries

1. Use the Reflection from the *Student Book*. Students could compare and evaluate their outcomes.
2. Any of the issues covered in the *Student Book* could be used as the basis for a class debate, either from a Hindu perspective or a more general view. For example: 'Hindus who engage in animal research or who eat meat are storing up karmic debt', 'Meat is murder', 'Animal acts in circuses should be illegal': do you agree or disagree?
3. Ask students, in groups, to create an 'Animal Rules' chart, using ideas from the *Student Book* activities. The aim is to demonstrate an understanding of key teachings and how they can apply to daily life.

Further class and homework activities

1. Both 4.6 Animals Interactive Activity and 4.6 Ganesha Worksheet (which provides students with a formal answer space for the question that accompanies the image of Ganesha in the *Student Book*) on the *Hinduism OxBox Online* could be completed as plenaries, by reviewing and discussing the answers in a class context.
2. Further suggestions on page 76 of this book.

4.7 Planet or People? Caring for the Environment

The unit in brief

This unit introduces some Hindu teachings about respect for the Earth. Individuals in the case studies share their personal attitudes to the environment and the reasons for their views.

Key ideas

- Some scientific and religious ideas about the environment
- How environmental concerns go beyond faith and culture
- Students' own impact on the Earth's resources
- The pros and cons of technological advancement

Useful Word

carbon footprint

Skills practised

- Literacy: interpreting quotations from Hindu scripture
- Thinking: analysing and evaluating ideas about the importance of the Earth in relation to humans
- Personal reflection: thinking about own impact upon the environment
- Applying learning to life: looking at ways to reduce own impact upon the environment

Resources

- 4.7 Environment Film Clip A: the Patani family speaks about 'being green'
- 4.7 Environment Film Clip B: the Morris family speaks about the environment
- 4.7 Earth Interactive Activity: students fill the gaps in a paragraph to assess their understanding of the unit
- 4.7 Film Worksheet: students assess their understanding of the case study film clips by linking ideas to the *Student Book*
- 4 Image Gallery: a useful gallery of photos and film stills from the chapter
- 4.7 Lesson Player: a ready-to-go presentation with built-in resources and teacher notes
- 4.7 Self-Assessment Sheet: students evaluate their learning against the lesson objectives

Ideas for starters

1. Use the starter in the *Student Book*.
2. Share a series of images with students. For each series, ask students to note the first three words that come to mind and any questions they have. You could use:

- images showing the impact of global warming, for example, the melting ice caps
- images of natural beauty, for example, rainforests
- images of damage to the Earth caused by humans, for example, landfill sites and power stations.

3. Ask students to list or share in pairs three ways in which they show respect or care for the Earth and why they do this.

Activity guidance

- You might want to stage a class debate as a follow up to Activity **4** in the *Student Book*.
- This unit makes reference to Christian views about the environment. To compare this with Hindu views you could refer to Unit 5.4 in the *Christianity Student Book*.

Ideas for plenaries

1. Use the Reflection in the *Student Book*. You could ask students to share their reflections with a partner, or as a 'letter to Durga'.
2. Ask students to go to the 'How you can help' section of the World Wide Fund for Nature's (WWF's) website and follow the links to calculate their own carbon footprint. Ask them to discuss in pairs whether the result surprises them or not.
3. Ask students to role-play in pairs an interview with Nisha Patani about why she does her best to take care of the Earth.

Further class and homework activities

1 Who does the Earth belong to?
   - **a)** Ask students to compose a post of 140 characters for a social network, which explains their view.
   - **b)** Students should research a range of responses to this question, from a range of belief systems, and present their findings as if it is a social network conversation with several different people commenting.

2. As a homework activity, students could investigate the work and mission statement of WWF or another environmental charity. Ask them to share their findings as a fact-file, newspaper or filmed report.
3. 4.7 Interactive Activity on the *Hinduism OxBox Online.*
4. 4.7 Environment Film Clips A and B on the *Hinduism OxBox Online.*
5. 4.7 Film Worksheet on the *Hinduism OxBox Online.*
6. Further suggestions on page 76 of this book.

Chapter 4 Further Suggestions

These suggestions are addressed directly to students.

4.1 The Four Aims in Life

1 What is your favourite sight, sound, smell, touch and taste? Consider what makes these so special. Is it *just* how they look/sound etc., or are there deeper reasons, e.g. a connection to a memory, person or place? Stop and think about how and why you use certain senses and whether they connect to your emotions too. */**/***

2 In a way, aiming for moksha is aiming for the end of your own existence as an individual. This is quite different to many other belief systems, where the aim of life is to live forever, such as in Christian and Islamic concepts of eternity in heaven. Which aim ('the end of individual existence' or 'eternal existence') do you think is the most convincing and why? Which is the most appealing? ***

4.2 How do I Decide What's Right? Difficult Decisions!

1 Find out what 'just war' theory involves and apply it to wars and conflicts that have taken place in the last 100 years. Create a chart to show clearly those wars or conflicts that you think qualify as 'just war', and those that do not. ***

2 The capital punishment debate is often in the news when there has been a particularly atrocious crime. Research arguments for and against executing people as punishment, including some religious views, and present your findings (and your own opinions with your reasons for them) as a chart or mind-map. */**/***

4.3 How do I Decide What's Right? Some Dilemmas of Modern Life

1 Create a collage or series of images (digital or drawn) to illustrate some of the moral dilemmas that young people in the UK might face. Include a catchy title. *

2 Homework: List or keep cuttings of issues in the media that are examples of moral problems. For example: 'Should doctors turn off the life-support machine of a critically ill baby?' or 'Is it a good or bad thing for celebrities to adopt babies from less-developed countries?' */**/***

3 Is it OK to break the rules to fit in with the crowd? Share your thoughts as a personal diary entry or a blog. **/***

4.4 Are You What You Eat?

1 Many Hindus fast on different days of the week to show devotion to particular deities. Investigate some of the deities and fast days and create a 'Weekly Fasts Chart' that describes the deity and type of fast associated with each day of the week. */ **/***

2 'We all have a moral responsibility to take care of our health. The NHS is at breaking point and cannot keep paying for conditions that we create through our own bad choices, such as drink-related illnesses and type 2 diabetes (largely caused by obesity)'. Compose your own response to this statement, showing that you can see both sides of the debate – and include religious and moral reasoning to support your conclusions. ***

4.5 Special Feature: Food Glorious Food!

1 Investigate some health-giving foods traditionally recommended in Ayurveda, but now also recommended by some doctors and health experts, e.g. cinnamon, ginger, mint, garlic, turmeric, liquorice. Create a chart, PowerPoint presentation or poster that describes the possible benefits of each item and how to use it. */**/***

4.6 Animal Magic

1 Design an advert (film or poster) for the RSPCA or WWF with the aim of securing charitable donations made specifically to appeal to Hindus (i.e. include quotations or reasons which link to Hindu teachings). */**/***

2 Many Hindus consider it a daily duty to feed wild animals. Is this something you ever do? Reflect on your reasons why or why not. */**/***

4.7 Planet or People? Caring for the Environment

1 Investigate the work of ARC – the Alliance of Religions and Conservation – a multi-faith organization that works with WWF to help preserve the planet. Present your findings as a PowerPoint presentation or poster. */**/***

2 'ARC and similar projects are a waste of time; humans are on to road to self-destruction and it's too late to stop it now!'

a Prepare a set of questions to raise with people who hold this view. **/***

b Compose a speech to either support or argue against the view. ***

Chapter 4 Assessment

Assessment in the *Student Book*

You will find an assessment task at the end of every chapter which focuses on AT2. In this chapter, the task asks students to produce an in-depth investigative news report into one of the moral issues featured in the chapter, exploring Hindu views as well as their own and others.

In the *Student Book* (and on the supporting worksheets), you'll find guidance about levels of assessment that you can use to help your students understand what their work should include. You could ask them to use these criteria for self-or peer-assessment once they've completed the task.

Living Faiths Assessment

Student Book

- Assessment Task
- Levels Guidance

OxBox Online

- Auto-Marked Test
- Assessment Task Presentation
- Assessment Worksheets

Assessment Task for Chapter 4 (pages **62–63** of the *Hinduism Student Book*)

Objectives

- Explore and evaluate a moral issue from Hindu and other perspectives
- Use reasoning and evidence to inform your conclusions
- Explain a range of views as well as justify your own

Task

Your challenge is to produce an in-depth investigative news report into one of the moral issues featured in this chapter. Make sure that you include Hindu perspectives as well as your own point of view. Use different ways to present information, so that it's visually engaging and inviting to read, for example, graphs, maps, diagrams, speech bubbles or information files.

Assessment in *OxBox Online*

On the *Hinduism OxBox Online*, you'll find resources to use when introducing the assessment task to the class.

You can use the *Chapter 4 Assessment Task Presentation* as a front-of-class tool to help your students unpack the assessment criteria, and understand what is expected of them.

Chapter 4 Assessment Worksheets accompany the task, so that once you finish the presentation, your students can easily get started.

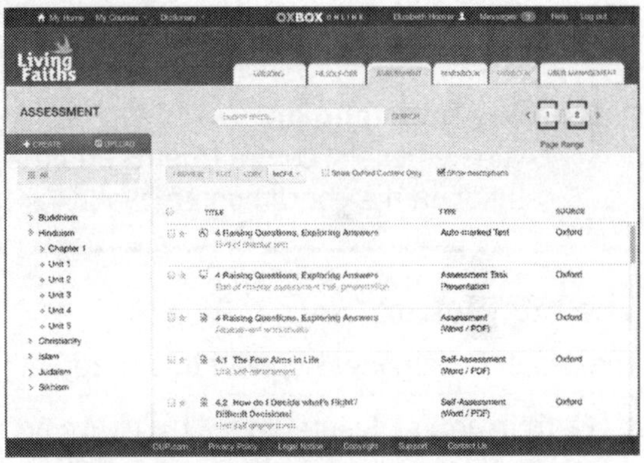

▲ Assessment resources for Chapter 4 on the *Hinduism Oxbox Online*

Auto-marked tests

The *Hinduism OxBox Online* also contains auto-marked tests for each chapter to help save you time setting questions and marking for AT1. The test for this chapter contains 15 questions and will take most students about half an hour. Test results are automatically stored in the markbook.

Digital markbook

A markbook and a reporting function complete the *OxBox Online* assessment package, so you can keep all your students' test results and assessment scores in one place. This can include the auto-marked tests as well as pieces of work you or the students have marked by hand.

Chapter 5 Overview
Hindu Beliefs in Action

Helping you deliver Key Stage 3 RE

This chapter addresses the following areas of the Programme of Study:

Key concepts

Identity, diversity and belonging

- Explore the variety, difference and relationships that exist within and between religions, values and beliefs

Practices and ways of life

- Explore the impact of religions and beliefs on how people live their lives
- Understand that religious practices are diverse, change over time and are influenced by cultures

Key processes

Learning about religion

- Investigate the impact of religious beliefs and teachings on individuals, communities and societies, the reasons for commitment and the causes of diversity

Learning from religion

- Evaluate beliefs, commitments and the impact of religion in the contemporary world

The big picture

These are the key ideas behind this chapter:

- Faith in action. Many Hindus try to live according to the concept of sewa (service), which means actively trying to serve others. Getting involved in Hindu charities, such as Sewa UK, is one way that they can do this.
- As well as the usual pressures experienced by people when choosing careers, Hindus have the added consideration of exploring careers that will fulfill dharma (duty). Many feel that they have to consider their moral values and religious teachings when thinking about doing certain jobs.
- Cultural confusion. As with other faiths, there are many issues in Hinduism where religious and cultural teachings are often mixed up or misunderstood, e.g. arranged marriage, gender equality and politics. There are a wide range of Hindu groups holding differing viewpoints.

Chapter outline

Use this to give students a mental road map of the chapter:

5.1 Sewa is Service – focusses on the work and philosophy of Sewa UK, and how they 'live' the concept of sewa

5.2 What Shall I Do? Dharma and Career Choices – uses case studies to examine the issue of career choice for Hindus today

5.3 What about Relationships? – examines the Hindu wedding ceremony and ideas about arranged marriage

5.4 Girls Allowed! The Role of Women in Hinduism – examines Hindu teaching about gender roles in theory and in practice

5.5 Militant Hinduism? – explores the issues of militancy and liberalism as they relate to Hinduism, including the principle of ahimsa in practice

5.6 Faith on Faith: Sharing with the Community – discusses the sharing of faith, including interfaith activity

Opportunities for assessment

Summative assessments on the *Hinduism OxBox Online* include auto-marked tests, interactive activities, and self-assessment worksheets.

The end-of-chapter assessment task in the *Student Book* provides formative assessment. Supporting materials for the assessment task can be found on the *Hinduism OxBox Online*, such as the Assessment Task Presentation and the related worksheets.

There are other opportunities for assessment too. For example, you could use some of the activities or reflection points throughout each *Student Book* unit, or some of the 'Further Suggestions' at the end of this chapter.

Getting ready for this chapter

- If possible, invite members of the local Hindu community to come into school and share how their faith affects their career choice/options, or watch 5.2 Careers Film Clip A on the *Hinduism OxBox Online.*

- Look out for any current issues where Hindu views conflict within the faith or with the wider community (e.g. the debate about open air cremation in the UK).

Objectives and outcomes for this chapter

Objectives	Unit	Outcomes
Most students will:		Most students will be able to:
• develop an understanding of the meaning of sewa, and also investigate the work of Sewa UK • explore what motivates charity volunteers • evaluate the value of sewa and Sewa UK in the modern world.	**5.1**	• give examples of some ways in which the charity Sewa UK works • explain a range of reasons why people may choose to help a charity • explain their own views about the concept of service and the value of charities such as Sewa.
• expand their understanding of dharma • analyse what makes a career fulfilling • reflect upon their own and others' career aspirations.	**5.2**	• apply learning from previous lessons to this unit • give examples of fulfilling jobs and explain why they are not 'just' money-making careers • identify a range of reasons why they and others may wish to do a certain job (and the merits/downfalls of those careers).
• develop an understanding of the connections between some ancient and modern Hindu beliefs and practices • investigate and evaluate arranged marriage in Hinduism • consider how Hindus might interpret scripture in different ways.	**5.3**	• make connections between eros in Hindu scripture and the modern world, and about reasons for marriage and the way people meet partners • Explain some of the reasons why arranged marriage exists in Hindu culture • relate different interpretations of Hindu scripture to the subject of marriage.
• evaluate the roles of women in Hindu culture • identify and discuss differences between religious teaching and social practice • explore and explain their own views about male and female roles.	**5.4**	• identify similarities and differences between the traditional views of women in Hindu and British culture • give examples of, and reasons for, some Hindus worshipping Devi but not allowing 'real' women equal status to men • justify whether they believe gender equality is a reality, possibility or impossibility.
• examine and explain some of the areas of conflict between Hindus, and also between some Hindus and other groups • evaluate some difficult issues about respect and tolerance.	**5.5**	• identify and explain some issues where some Hindus disagree with each other, or with other groups • 'see both sides' of the debate regarding areas of conflict and justify their own views using moral and/or religious reasoning.
• evaluate the importance of interfaith activity • identify ways people may learn from faith • analyse their own and other people's reasons and actions in sharing beliefs.	**5.6**	• give reasons for and against holding interfaith dialogue and events • give examples of a range of ways in which Hindus may share their faith with each other and with others • evaluate the pros and cons of sharing your faith.

5.1 Sewa is Service

The unit in brief

This unit explores the Hindu concept of sewa and connects it with the work of a Hindu charity (Sewa UK). There is also some consideration of the different motivations that people may have for helping others, and why there is a need for sewa in the world.

Key ideas

- The meaning of sewa
- What motivates charity volunteers
- The value of sewa, and the work of the organization, Sewa UK, in the modern world

Useful Words

daya, non-governmental, non-sectarian, sewa

Skills practised

- Application of learning: using understanding of Hindu principles to draw conclusions
- Research: finding and using appropriate information from other faiths

Resources

- 5.1 Charity Interactive Activity A: students match terms from the unit to their correct definitions
- 5.1 Charity Interactive Activity B: students rank reasons for involvement in charity
- 5.1 Sewa Worksheet: students mind-map why sewa is important to Hindus
- 5 Image Gallery: a useful gallery of photos and film stills from the chapter
- 5.1 Lesson Player: a ready-to-go presentation with built-in resources and teacher notes
- 5.1 Self-Assessment Sheet: students evaluate their learning against the lesson objectives

Ideas for starters

1. Use the starter from the *Student Book*. You could ask if anyone in the class has written down the organization, Sewa UK, on their list. If 'yes', they could share with the class what they know about the charity, as a way into the unit.
2. Present a series of pictures featuring different examples of sewa (e.g. holding a door open for someone, disaster relief work, shaking a charity tin, doing a sponsored activity, caring for an elderly person) and ask students to decide what the connection between them is.

3. Distribute flyers for a range of charities or organizations that help other people. Ask students to list or discuss reasons why:
   a) anyone would join them or volunteer for them
   b) Hindus, in particular, may wish to join them or volunteer for them.

Activity guidance

- This unit invites students to compare the Hindu concept of sewa to the teachings of other faiths. See Unit 5.4 in the *Judaism Student Book*, or Unit 3.2 in the *Islam Student Book*.

Ideas for plenaries

1. Use the Reflection from the *Student Book*.
2. Ask students to choose one of the quotations from Hindu sacred texts in this unit. They should then:
   a) re-write the quotation in their own words,
   b) come up with arguments for and against the statement. For instance, for the quotation from Bhagavad Gita 3.8, students could counter the statement by arguing that sometimes, though well meant, too much action can cause further problems if the actions are not properly thought through.
3. Present students with the question: '"Charity begins at home." Is this just an excuse to be selfish, or absolutely true in the real world?'
   a) Ask them to show their understanding of both views through a two-way text message conversation, with each person in the conversation justifying one of the views.
   b) Now ask students to work out their own views about this question. They should create a scale from 1 to 5, where 1 is 'true' and 5 is 'selfish'. Before placing themselves on this scale, they should write three descriptions for the views that represent 2, 3 and 4 on the scale.

Further class and homework activities

1. Ask students to investigate the work and mission statement of another faith-based charity as homework. You could ask them to compare it to Sewa UK. Ask them to consider: 'Should all charities just join together and work as one big group? Why or why not?'
2. Students should learn the Useful Words and definitions explored in this *Student Book* unit for a quick quiz next lesson.
3. 5.1 Charity Interactive Activities A and B on the *Hinduism OxBox Online*.
4. 5.1 Sewa Worksheet on the *Hinduism OxBox Online*.
5. Further suggestions on page 92 of this book.

5.2 What Shall I Do? Dharma and Career Choices

The unit in brief:

This unit explores ways in which faith may affect career paths, and also reviews some key concepts studied in previous units. The concept of a fulfilling career is considered.

Key ideas

- Existing understanding of dharma is expanded and applied to 'real life' issues
- The elements that make a career fulfilling
- Students' and others' career ambitions and aspirations
- Existing understanding of karma is developed

Useful Word

dharma

Skills practised

- Analysis: understanding what makes a career fulfilliing and not just a means to make money
- Self-awareness: acknowledging and evaluating on motives for career ambitions

Resources

- 5.2 Aspirations Film Clip A: Dave family members discuss career aspirations and influences
- 5.2 Aspirations Film Clip B: the Morris family discusses careers
- 5.2 Dharma Interactive Activity: students consider whether career-based actions fulfil dharma
- 5.2 Film Worksheet: students assess their understanding of the case study film clips by linking ideas to the *Student Book*
- 5 Image Gallery: a useful gallery of photos and film stills from the chapter
- 5.2 Lesson Player: a ready-to-go presentation with built-in resources and teacher notes
- 5.2 Self-Assessment Sheet: students evaluate their learning against the lesson objectives

Ideas for starters

1. Use the starter from the *Student Book*. You could make this a whole-class activity by playing 'pass the ball' in groups. Give each group a soft ball or other object and set a timer for two minutes. Students pass the ball around the group, and the student holding the ball needs to complete the sentence: 'When I grow up, I want to be a [...] because [...]' The aim is not to be the student left with the ball when the timer goes off.

2. Ask students, in pairs, to remind each other what the terms 'varna', 'ashrama', 'dharma' and 'karma' mean. They could refer to the glossary at the back of the *Student Book*. This could be a timed discussion.
3. Give different groups of students a picture, or just the title, of a job. Have a range, e.g. nursing, construction work, banking, education, armed forces, entertainment.
   a) Ask the groups to list as many reasons as they can think of to explain why a person might want to do each job.
   b) This activity could be extended by asking students: 'How might this profession allow a Hindu to: (i) fulfill dharma; (ii) create good karma; (iii) pay karmic debt; and (iv) follow their varna?'

Activity guidance

- You could ask students to present and peer-assess the outcomes from Activity **1** in the *Student Book*.
- To complete Activity **3** in the *Student Book*, students will need to be reminded that Hindu castes traditionally dictate a particular career path (see Units 1.5 and 3.5).

Ideas for plenaries

1. Ask students to investigate Hindus in the public eye or local community – what professions are they most/least involved in? (This could be an extended research and numeracy task using the 2011 census.) Discuss or list possible reasons for this. How many are linked to faith? To culture? To other factors?
2. Ask any willing Hindu parents or members of the local community to come in to speak to the class (maybe a Q & A session?) about factors that have influenced their career choice(s). You could also work with the school careers service and ask for any visitors who come into school to inspire students towards certain career paths to also share any moral or religious influences on their own careers.

Further class and homework activities

1. As homework, ask students to discuss job and career choices with people they know. Did their beliefs about right and wrong affect their choice of career? How? Why or why not?
2. 5.2 Dharma Interactive Activity on the *Hinduism OxBox Online* would work well as a plenary for this unit.
3. 5.2 Aspirations Film Clips A and B on the *Hinduism OxBox Online*.
4. 5.2 Film Worksheet on the *Hinduism OxBox Online*.
5. Further suggestions on page 92 of this book.

5.3 What about Relationships?

The unit in brief

This unit investigates religious and cultural attitudes to love and marriage. The issue of arranged marriage is explored and evaluated in particular.

Key ideas

- Hindu ideas about love and marriage
- The origins of arranged marriage in Hinduism

Useful Words

fertility, shaadi

Skills practised

- Open-mindedness: being accepting of a range of views and ways of living
- Empathy: trying to understand a range of views and ways of living by 'putting yourself in their place'
- Communication: expressing own views intelligently and with maturity
- Self-awareness: acknowledging own feelings and reasons for them

Resources

- 5.3 Viewpoints Interactive Activity: students decide which opinion disagrees with arranged marriages
- 5.3 Wedding Worksheet: students must draw and label items used in a Hindu wedding
- 5 Image Gallery: a useful gallery of photos and film stills from the chapter
- 5.3 Lesson Player: a ready-to-go presentation with built-in resources and teacher notes
- 5.3 Self-Assessment Sheet: students evaluate their learning against the lesson objectives

Ideas for starters

1. Ask students to look at the image of Lord Shiva and Lady Parvati in the *Student Book*. Ask them what they think about the concept of gods being in love. How might this concept affect a Hindu's view of love? You could ask them to research the story of Shiva and Parvati as a follow up.
2. Ask students to work in pairs. They have five minutes to remind each other of and note down everything they have learned so far about Hinduism and the issues of love and marriage. (This activity can be 'stand alone' or followed by the task below.)
3. Ask students what they know about what different faiths have to say about love and marriage, and write their responses on the board. You could come back to their thoughts at the end of the lesson.

Activity guidance

- You might want to compare the topics covered in this unit with the teachings of other faiths. See Unit 5.2 in the *Christianity Student Book*. You may also like to investigate BBC Learning Zone's online clips regarding arranged marriage in Hinduism.

Ideas for plenaries

1. Ask students to demonstrate learning of this lesson by creating a mind-map of everything they now know about love and marriage in Hinduism.
2. Students could share the points they have identified in their mind-map from plenary **1** with a partner, or you could pick volunteers to share their ideas with the class.

Further class and homework activities

1. As homework following on from the activities on arranged marriage in the *Student Book*, students could ask their families to choose a celebrity partner for them. Who would it be and why? They should ask for a top three (with reasons) from which they have to choose one. It's pretend, but the point is whether the families use the same criteria and thinking as the students themselves. Discuss the reasons for any differences in views and choices – is it about different values, experience, or something else?
2. 5.3 Interactive Activity on the *Hinduism OxBox Online*.
3. 5.3 Wedding Worksheet on the *Hinduism OxBox Online*.
4. Further suggestions on page 92 of this book.

5.4 Girls Allowed! The Role of Women in Hinduism

The unit in brief

This unit examines the subject of female roles in Hinduism, including through case studies. Students also consider their own thoughts about gender roles in society today.

Key ideas

- The roles and place of women in Hindu culture
- Differences between Hindu religious teaching and social/cultural practice
- Students' own views about male and female roles and equality

Useful Words

devi, patriarchy, shakti

Skills practised

- Literacy: using new words correctly
- Social awareness: by 'opening up' the issues of patriarchy and gender inequality

Resources

- 5.4 Gender Film Clip A: Nisha Patani and her grandmother
- 5.4 Gender Film Clip B: Miran and his mother speak about male and female roles
- 5.4 Gender Film Clip C: Dave family members talking about gender issues and careers
- 5.4 Gender Film Clip D: Dave family members discuss gender inequality
- 5.4 Rhyme Audio Clip: the nursery rhyme, "What are little boys made of?"
- 5.4 Shakti Interactive Activity: students categorize the qualities of Shakti
- 5.4 Film Worksheet: students assess their understanding of the case study film clips by linking ideas to the *Student Book*
- 5 Image Gallery: a useful gallery of photos and film stills from the chapter
- 5.4 Lesson Player: a ready-to-go presentation with built-in resources and teacher notes
- 5.4 Self-Assessment Sheet: students evaluate their learning against the lesson objectives

Ideas for starters

1. Use 5.4 Rhyme Audio Clip to support this activity. Tell students to think about the nursery rhyme that suggests boys are made of 'slugs and snails and puppy dogs' tails' and girls are made of 'sugar and spice and all things nice'. What stereotypes does this rhyme promote?
2. Ask students to choose a man and a woman who they admire in the media. Students should list their qualities and explain why they admire these people.
3. Present a range of images of men and women (including both stereotypes and challenges to stereotypes, e.g. a woman putting on make-up and a man cooking).

a) Ask students to rate the images as 'positive', 'negative' or 'neutral'.
b) Share and compare responses. Is there a gender division within the group about how the images are perceived?
c) Discuss possible reasons for any different perceptions.

Ideas for plenaries

1. Share and compare responses to Activity **4** in the *Student Book*. Does most of the class see it as 'remaining' or 'down', or is it even? Discuss reasons for any different perceptions.
2. Ask students to carry out research and create a social networking profile for a Hindu goddess of their choice. They need to include key facts, qualities and stories.
3. Ask students to investigate 'The first person to...'. For example, the first person to: climb Mount Everest, drive a car in the UK, send a text message, sail around the world single-handed, run 100m in under ten seconds. How many of those people chosen are men and how many are women? Explore what factors affect these statistics, e.g. biology, physique, social and educational opportunities, financial factors. Do students conclude that, historically, women have been restricted by cultural views about gender, or not?

Further class and homework activities

1. 5.4 Shakti Interactive Activity on the *Hinduism OxBox Online* would work well as a plenary for this unit.
2. 5.4 Gender Film Clips A, B, C and D on the *Hinduism OxBox Online.*
3. 5.4 Film Worksheet on the *Hinduism OxBox Online* .
4. Further suggestions on page 92 of this book.

5.5 Militant Hinduism?

The unit in brief

This unit explains key terms linked to the issue of militancy. It also explores issues causing conflict among Hindus, and between Hindus and other groups.

Key ideas

- Reasons why some Hindus have a militant response to faith issues
- Reasons why many Hindus have a liberal response to faith issues

Useful Words

liberal, militant, secular

Skills practised

- Enquiry: finding out more and asking intelligent questions
- Empathy: trying to see things from someone else's perspective
- Problem solving: using reasoning and thinking skills to find a solution
- Communication: expressing views with maturity and creativity

Resources

- 5.5 Terms Interactive Activity: students must match terms covered in this unit to their correct definitions
- 5.5 Poster Worksheet: students create a poster as a possible way of completing Activity 2 in the *Student Book*
- 5 Image Gallery: a useful gallery of photos and film stills from the chapter
- 5.5 Lesson Player: a ready-to-go presentation with built-in resources and teacher notes
- 5.5 Self-Assessment Sheet: students evaluate their learning against the lesson objectives

Ideas for starters

1. Use the starter in the *Student Book*. You could ask students whether they know of any examples of ongoing religious conflict in the news.
2. Present images of a range of 'militant' and 'liberal' activities or protest groups. Ask students to:
   a) separate the images into two groups – 'militant' and 'liberal'
   b) identify what the common factor is for each group.
3. Ask students to 'think, pair, share' what they understand the saying 'one man's meat is another man's poison' to mean. Use the discussion as a lead in to how some Hindus might be highly offended or angered by things which other Hindus might not be bothered about, or may even actively support.

Activity guidance

- With Activity **1** in the *Student Book*, you could keep a note of the issues raised across all the pairs. Overall, do there seem to be more reasons to stock and sell goods with Hindu deities on them or not?
- For Activity **2** in the *Student Book* or the worksheet for this unit, you might want to compare stances and ask: 'Which side has the most support? Why?' Students could also consider outcomes from a skills angle: 'Which side is most effectively communicated? What are the strengths and weaknesses of the speeches/posters/leaflets?'
- On the topic of the protests against the Australian designer, Lisa Blue, you could find an original news article (for example on The Telegraph's website) and ask students whether they agree that the official apology offered by the design company was necessary.

Ideas for plenaries

1. Choose other issues that are debated by Hindus. For example, a minority of Hindus in the UK wants to legalize open-air funeral pyres. Ask students to consider what they would decide if they were the judge in one of these cases. You could decide the issue either by holding a class vote or a class debate. Those who have a strong view either way should go to different ends of the room and have the challenge of getting the 'undecided' to join their side.
2. Some people believe that the answer to friction between religions is just to ban religion. For example, French law forbids any religious symbols or clothing/jewellery in schools on the grounds that this makes everyone the same, and because 'religion is a personal, not a public matter'.

   The question: Should Britain introduce a similar law to that in France?

   Ask students to demonstrate their thinking skills, application of learning and understanding of differences within Hinduism by answering the question:
   a) from the point of view of a militant Hindu
   b) from the point of view of a liberal Hindu
   c) as themselves.

Further class and homework activities

1. Before teaching this unit, you could use 5 Image Gallery on *Hinduism OxBox Online* to show students the image of the Australian designer protest and ask them what they think is happening. This could be a good introduction to the Starter in the *Student Book*, which asks in what situations might people become angry for a religious reason.
2. 5.5 Terms Interactive Activity on the *Hinduism OxBox Online*.
3. 5.5 Poster Worksheet on the *Hinduism OxBox Online*.
4. Further suggestions on page 92 of this book.

5.6 Faith on Faith: Sharing with the Community

The unit in brief

This unit explores ways in which Hindus, including those featured in case studies, share their faith through daily life and celebrations. Interfaith work is also analysed and evaluated.

Key ideas

- Ways in which Hindus share their faith
- Evaluating the value of interfaith activity

Useful Words

convert, evangelism/evangelical, interfaith, ISKCON, mission

Skills practised

- Thinking: analysing and evaluating issues covered in the unit
- Communication: sharing and justifying views

Resources

- 5.6 Mantra Audio Clip: Gaiatri recites a mantra
- 5.6 Sharing Faith Film Clip A: Nisha and Nirav Patani discuss sharing faith
- 5.6 Sharing Faith Film Clip B: Gaiatri talks about collective worship
- 5.6 Terms Interactive Activity: students link key words from the unit to their definitions
- 5.6 Film Worksheet: students assess their understanding of the case study clips by linking ideas to the *Student Book*
- 5 Image Gallery: a useful gallery of photos and film stills from the chapter
- 5.6 Lesson Player: a ready-to-go presentation with built-in resources and teacher notes
- 5.6 Self-Assessment Sheet: students evaluate their learning against the lesson objectives

Ideas for starters

1. Use the starter in the *Student Book*.
2. If possible, show the video of Hindus singing in the streets of London on the home page of the ISKCON website. Ask students to make a list of questions to ask the people in the film in order to find out more about what they are doing and why.
3. Ask students to list as many examples of religious symbols or dress across different beliefs as they can. Ask them to note or say what each symbol or item of religious dress tells others about the wearer's beliefs.

4. Think, pair, share: 'How do other people know what you believe?'. Consider actions and symbols as well as what you say. Encourage feedback that stretches students to realize that what they read, eat, the places they go to, the TV programmes they love or hate, and the 'celebs' they admire or dislike, might all indicate their beliefs.

Activity guidance

You might want to compare Hindu beliefs on this topic with those of other faiths. See Unit 5.6 in the *Christianity Student Book* or Unit 5.6 in the *Sikhism Student Book*.

Ideas for plenaries

1. Ask students to make an 'agree and disagree' chart in response to the statement: 'Faith is a personal matter and should only be shared with other believers'.
2. Ask students to imagine that they are Hindus living in France. Ask them to compose an email or record a message to send to friends in the UK explaining how the French law about sharing faith in school (see *Teacher Guide* Unit 5.5) causes them no/some/major difficulty in practising their faith.
3. Ask students to investigate cases of people claiming that their human right to freely practise their religion was denied by their employer/school/the UK justice system because they were not allowed to wear faith symbols and/or clothing associated with their faith to work or school. Ask students how they would have judged these cases and why.
4. Ask students to plan an event at school where people can share and learn about different faiths. Who would they invite? What topics should speakers cover?

Further class and homework activities

1. If possible, invite Hindus in the local area to visit the school and explain how they share their faith with others.
2. 5.6 Interactive Activity on the *Hinduism OxBox Online* would work well as a plenary.
3. 5.6 Sharing Faith Film Clips A and B on the *Hinduism OxBox Online*. Show students these clips and ask: 'What is the main feeling you get from these clips? Curiosity? Fun? Bewilderment? Empathy? Something else?'
4. 5.6 Film Worksheet on the *Hinduism OxBox Online*.
5. Play 5.6 Mantra Audio Clip on the *Hinduism OxBox Online*, so students can experience the mantra Gaiatri recited at school.
6. Further suggestions on page 92 of this book.

Chapter 5 Further Suggestions

These suggestions are addressed directly to students.

5.1 Sewa is Service

1 Investigate the work and mission statements of at least one other faith-based charity (other than Sewa UK) and present your findings as a PowerPoint presentation or booklet. **/***

2 Some charities that originally began as religious organizations have since become secular (non-religious), e.g. Oxfam and The Red Cross. List or mind-map possible reasons for this. ***

3 If you do not already give up some time to helping others or the environment, challenge yourself to do something for at least a term. It could involve working with a local group or even just helping out at home more.

5.2 What Shall I Do? Dharma and Career Choices

1 **a** Survey others in your class about what job they would like to do when they are older and present the results as a pie chart or bar graph. */**

b Comment on the range and popularity of career choices in the class in the form of a newspaper front page that presents and analyses your survey results. You will also need to think of an attention-grabbing headline and use a range of communication methods, e.g. interviews and feature boxes. ***

5.3 What about Relationships?

1 **a** Make an invitation card for a Hindu wedding, using your understanding of the key symbols and features involved. */**

b Highlight which features are religious and which are cultural. You will need to research several websites or textbooks, not just one, to get a range of features and practices. **/***

2 **a** Marriage between Hindus and partners from different religious and secular backgrounds is increasing. The couple quite often have a Hindu wedding ceremony as part, or even the whole, of their marriage ritual. This means that it is OK for those with different beliefs to take part in a Hindu wedding ceremony.

b Do you think that a Hindu wedding ceremony is mostly a religious or mostly a cultural ritual? Why is it OK for non-Hindus to have a Hindu wedding, when some faiths require both partners to be from that faith? Support your reasoning with examples (pictures may be used as well as words) and reference to previous learning. ***

5.4 Girls Allowed! The Role of Women in Hinduism

1 There are many pairings like Lord Shiva and Lady Parvati among the Hindu deities. Research at least three more and identify features associated with each deity */**/***

2 Prepare a speech or presentation, or design a poster, which gets across to young people that gender should not be a bar to anything. Remember that this applies to boys having the freedom to engage in traditionally female pursuits, as well as the other way round. Use examples from Hindu teachings, deities or famous people to support the message. */**/ ***

5.5 Militant Hinduism?

1 Investigate one area of discord between faiths, or groups, in some detail (e.g. Northern Ireland, Palestine, for and against fox-hunting or vivisection) and make a 'Rough Guide to ...' about the issue. It should include your views about what the *main* reasons for the intolerance are. In particular, consider the influence of politics and upbringing on people. ***

2 Is there anything that you would protest about (like the deity images on swimwear issue in the *Student Book*)? Reflect on reasons for your passion, or lack of it, and communicate your thoughts as a diary entry (e.g. 'Dear diary, I am SO angry about… because…' or 'Dear Diary, all my friends are SO upset about… but I don't feel as strongly because…') **/***

5.6 Faith on Faith: Sharing with the Community

1 Plan a 'One World' festival that celebrates all people and beliefs. */**/***

2 Religious practice was (and is) banned in some countries around the world.

a Imagine how it would be to have no religious celebrations of any kind. Would it bring people together or separate them? **

b In most of the countries that once banned religion, but now allow it, a lot of people have strong religious beliefs. How and why do you think these beliefs survived years of being banned? Share your thoughts as a mind-map or magazine article. ***

Chapter 5 Assessment

Assessment in the *Student Book*

You will find an assessment task at the end of every chapter which focuses on AT2. In this chapter, the task asks students to imagine they are an Agony Aunt or Uncle, and write three 'reader' letters along with responses that demonstrate understanding of some ways in which Hindus may respond to their beliefs.

In the *Student Book* (and on the supporting worksheets), you'll find guidance about levels of assessment that you can use to help your students understand what their work should include. You could ask them to use these criteria for self or peer assessment once they've completed the task.

Living Faiths Assessment

Student Book

- Assessment Task
- Levels Guidance

OxBox Online

- Auto-Marked Test
- Assessment Task Presentation
- Assessment Worksheets

Assessment Task for Chapter 5 (pages **76–77** of the *Hinduism Student Book*)

Objectives

- Demonstrate insight and understanding of some ways in which Hindus may respond to their beliefs
- Evaluate beliefs, commitments and the impact of some Hindus' views in the contemporary world
- Understand that although religious and cultural values are separate, they may be confused both by Hindus and others

Task

You are the Agony Aunt/Uncle for the new UK Teen website 'Young Hindu'. Because it's just launched, you've been asked to invent three letters to give readers a flavour of the kind of questions that they could email or text you about. You will have to provide answers as well as make up the problems!

Assessment in *OxBox Online*

On the *Hinduism OxBox Online*, you'll find resources to use when introducing the assessment task to the class.

You can use the *Chapter 5 Assessment Task Presentation* as a front-of-class tool to help your students unpack the assessment criteria, and understand what is expected of them.

Chapter 5 Assessment Worksheets accompany the task, so that once you finish the presentation, your students can easily get started.

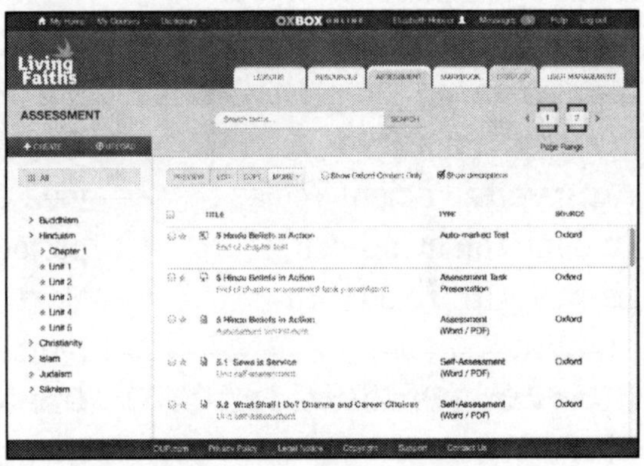

▲ Assessment resources for Chapter 5 on the *Hinduism Oxbox Online*

Auto-marked tests

The *Hinduism OxBox Online* also contains auto-marked tests for each chapter to help save you time setting questions and marking for AT1. The test for this chapter contains 15 questions and will take most students about half an hour. Test results are automatically stored in the markbook.

Digital markbook

A markbook and a reporting function complete the OxBox Online assessment package, so you can keep all your students' test results and assessment scores in one place. This can include the auto-marked tests as well as pieces of work you or the students have marked by hand.

Glossary

Afterlife Some kind of existence after death
Agape Love for the world and humanity
Ahimsa The Hindu principle of total non-violence in thoughts, words and actions
Artha Earning wealth honestly
Aryan An ancient race from what is now India/Iran
Ashrama The four main stages of life in Hinduism
Atheism An absence of belief in the Divine
Atheist A person who does not believe in the existence of the Divine
Atman The Hindu term for the eternal part of a person
Aum The symbol of Hinduism, meaning 'the eternal sound'
Avatar (incarnation) the Divine in human (or animal) form
Ayurveda Ancient Vedic guidance on living well
Ayurvedic To do with Ayurveda
Bhagvan A Hindu word for the Divine
Bhajan The term for sacred songs and also for an event where such songs are sung
Bhakti Devotion and ritual
Carbon footprint The environmental cost and consequences of how we live
Caste A system of social classes in Hindu culture, based on the roles that people play in society
Convert To persuade someone to change their beliefs
Cyclical time Time with many beginnings and many ends
Daya Compassion for all living things
Deity A god or goddess (the Divine)
Devi Hindu word for goddess
Dharma Duty; purpose in life
Disciple A devoted follower
The Divine The highest spirit beyond this world (God or gods/goddesses)
Eros Romantic love
Eternal Lasting forever, with no beginning or end
Ethics/ethical To do with right and wrong
Euthanasia Helping someone else to die
Evangelism/evangelical Spreading a faith
Extended family The wider family group, including aunts, uncles, cousins and close friends
Fast/fasting To go without food, or some foods, for a set period of time
Fertility The ability to reproduce
Gnaan Wisdom gained from scholarly research and meditation
Guna The Hindu word for the (good and bad) qualities and characteristics of a person
Guru The Sanskrit word for teacher or master
Infinite Endless or eternal
Interfaith Between faiths
ISKCON International Society for Krishna Consciousness
Janmashtami A celebration of Lord Krishna's birthday
Kama Achieving rightful desires of the senses through action
Karma The concept that your actions, and those of others, have consequences
Karmic debt The payment (in deeds or suffering) that is a consequence of bad karma
Liberal Open to new ideas and willing to accept differences and changes
Linear time There is a point at which time began and a point when it will end
Mandir The proper term for a Hindu temple
Mantra A sacred phrase or prayer, usually chanted during worship or meditation
Mata Literally, 'mother', but also used as the term for female gurus
Militant Unwilling to tolerate the beliefs of others and willing to resort to violence
Mission What a person or group aims for
Moksha Believed by many Hindus to be the ultimate goal of all souls; becoming one with the Supreme Spirit
Monotheism Belief in only one God
Moral About what is right and wrong
Moral dilemma A situation where all of the options you face have something wrong about them
Morality A person's sense of right and wrong
Narg The Hindu term for hell
Non-governmental Not linked to any political party or government

Non-sectarian All religions and beliefs (including atheism) are accepted
Pantheism Belief that the Divine is everywhere and everything is divine
Patriarchy A system where the father figure is in charge
Philos Love for family and friends
Pluralism More than one form of, or idea about, the Divine can exist and be true at the same time
Polytheism Belief in many gods and goddesses
Prejudice Making often-negative judgements about a person without knowing them
Puja Personal or communal (group) worship
Rajas/rajasic Passion/passionate or greedy
Raksha Bandhan A festival where sisters give a rakhi to their brothers as a symbol of love and protection
Reincarnation A cycle of birth, existence, death and rebirth
Religious founder A person who is the starting point of a faith
Ritual An action or set of actions performed in a certain way, often as part of worship
Sacred texts Another name for books that are considered to be holy and to contain divine wisdom
Sanatan Dharma This literally means 'eternal laws' and is the 'real' term for Hinduism
Sattva/sattvic Purity/pure
Scripture Writing; often used to refer to religious writing
Secular Without religious reference; non-religious
Sewa Service to others and the world
Shaadi Hindi word for Marriage
Shakti A word literally meaning 'strength' or 'energy'; also a term for the feminine aspects of the Divine
Shruti 'heard'; a term used for the oldest Hindu texts, believed to have been directly spoken to rishis (wise ones) and seen as 'divine wisdom'
Smriti 'remembered'; a term used for scriptures providing structured guidelines for life, based on the 'divine wisdom', and originally passed through 'word of mouth' from guru to disciple
Spiritual fulfilment Feeling complete, having a real purpose in life
Storge Love for a place, activity or object
Sustainable Does not use all of something up; can be continued for a long time
Swami A guru, usually male, who has entered the fourth ashrama (that of holy person)
Swarg The Hindu term for heaven
Swastika An ancient symbol associated with many groups; it is used as a symbol of good luck in many areas of Hindu worship
Tamas/tamasic Lethargy/lethargic or lazy
Theist A person who believes in the existence of the Divine
Varna The Hindu word for caste
Varnashrama dharma The duties that must be completed in order to attain moksha
Vedic From the Hindu scriptures, the Vedas

OXFORD
UNIVERSITY PRESS

Great Clarendon Street, Oxford OX2 6DP

Oxford University Press is a department of the University of Oxford. It furthers the University's objective of excellence in research, scholarship, and education by publishing worldwide in

Oxford New York

Auckland Cape Town Dar es Salaam Hong Kong Karachi Kuala Lumpur Madrid Melbourne Mexico City Nairobi New Delhi Shanghai Taipei Toronto

With offices in

Argentina Austria Brazil Chile Czech Republic France Greece Guatemala Hungary Italy Japan Poland Portugal Singapore South Korea Switzerland Thailand Turkey Ukraine Vietnam

Oxford is a registered trade mark of Oxford University Press in the UK and in certain other countries

First published 2013

British Library Cataloguing in Publication Data

Data available

ISBN-13: 978-0-19-912998-0

10 9 8 7 6 5 4 3 2 1

Printed by Bell & Bain Ltd, Glasgow

Acknowledgements

The publishers would like to thank the following for permissions to use their photographs:

Cover: Godong/Robert Harding/Rex Features; All other photos by OUP

From the author, Neera Vyas: Love and thanks to my dear and wise mum for answering phone calls at all times of the day (and night!) and helping me with all areas of the project. Also to my poor abandoned daughter, for patience and understanding way beyond most adults, let alone most six- year-olds!

OUP wishes to thank the Patani, Dave and Morris families for agreeing to take part in the case study films and to be photographed for this title.